AI Tech Secrets

AI TECH SECRETS

Grow Your Income, Impact, and Productivity with AI and Web Strategies

Steve Klein

Wooded Creek
Publishing

AI Tech Secrets
Grow Your Income, Impact, and Productivity with AI and Web Strategies.

ISBN 978-0-9988270-1-8 - *paperback*

Published by Wooded Creek Publishing, a subsidiary of Zareco, Inc.

This book is dedicated to the leaders, professionals, and organizations driving meaningful transformation through the thoughtful application of AI and web-based systems. Your commitment to innovation, operational excellence, and strategic growth continues to inspire my work. Whether navigating complex challenges or building resilient digital infrastructure, you are laying the foundation for the next era of intelligent business. It's a privilege to contribute to that journey alongside you.

Contents

Introduction: Unlocking the Power of AI and the Web 13

1: The AI Advantage The Future of Online Success 19

2: Web-Based Tools for Wealth - Essential AI Tools 35

3: The AI Web Accelerator Framework - Move Fast Strategy . 47

4: Leveraging AI for Massive Productivity Gains 59

5: Building a Powerful Online Brand Using AI 83

6: Creating Wealth with AI-Generated Products 97

7: Real-World Results - Case Studies and Success Stories . 113

8: AI Isn't Perfect, But It's Close Enough 131

9: Navigating AI's Agreeability Bias – The Echo Chamber... 147

10: Debunking AI Myths – Embracing the Future 169

11: The AI Entrepreneur's Toolkit - for Success 187

12: The Future of AI—Staying Ahead of the Curve 211

Conclusion 237

About The Author 243

INTELLIGENT SYSTEMS AT EVERY LEVEL

While many of the examples in this book reference small teams, creators, and individual professionals, the underlying principles apply equally to large organizations, leadership teams, and enterprise systems navigating AI-driven change.

The focus throughout is not on tools, trends, or tactics, but on how intelligent systems reshape communication, decision-making, and operational structure at every level.

Introduction: Unlocking the Power of AI and the Web

Have you ever wanted to get more out of life? You might be a driven professional with big ideas, or an entrepreneur already achieving some success. But like many of us, you may also feel there are more goals you want to pursue—yet never enough time or resources to make them happen.

For years, I found myself in that exact position. As a high-tech entrepreneur and software engineer, I'd worked with AI to help companies and clients achieve remarkable results. Through websites, software tools, and custom solutions, I'd helped businesses reach eight- and nine-figure milestones. But while I was immersed in their success, I was struggling to find the time and freedom to explore my own projects.

That was, until I discovered the power of specific AI and web tools. These tools transformed the way I worked, giving me a kind of "superpower" that allowed me to do more in less time, without a large team or budget. What once took me ten hours could now be done in two. Tasks that stretched across days could be finished in a single afternoon. It was like I'd suddenly unlocked a whole new world of possibilities.

One of the first AI tools I discovered helped me take an entire podcast transcript and turn it into a concise, search-optimized social media post in minutes. Gone were the hours of struggling to stay consistent online—this tool made it possible to stay active, visible, and engaged with my audience effortlessly. And that was just the beginning. Another AI-powered tool I found allowed me to create high-quality branding materials—from logos to marketing visuals—without the need for a professional designer. I could maintain a polished, cohesive brand identity without the delays or costs of outsourcing.

This newfound freedom of design and expression—without incurring extra costs—allowed my team and me at our media company to produce and implement logo designs seamlessly into our website development projects for clients. This saved valuable time for both our clients and us while greatly enhancing the services we provide.

With these tools, I was also able to take on a side project—a personal initiative I'd always wanted to try. Without a full team to help, I tested out new ideas, built a podcast, launched an online course, and expanded my reach across social media. In short, I was able to get the work of six people done with just myself and one team member—and in a fraction of the time and cost it would have required otherwise.

Not only did I see a nearly 200% revenue increase that year, but I also experienced the ultimate benefit: freedom from burnout and the ability to focus on high-impact tasks. The "mundane" was automated, leaving me to pursue bigger goals, and the results were beyond what I could have imagined.

And now, I want to share this approach with you. In this book, I'll introduce you to the tools, techniques, and web strategies that changed my life and my business. Whether you're looking to save time, increase productivity, or grow your brand and income online, the methods I'll share are designed to help you achieve results.

In the following chapters, we'll dive into the essentials:

- **Chapter 1: The AI Advantage—Why AI is the Future of Online Success**
  Discover why AI is not just a trend but a game-changing tool for maximizing your potential online and staying competitive in a rapidly evolving world.
- **Chapter 2: Web-Based Tools for Wealth—The Essential AI Tools You Need**
  Explore the must-have AI tools that can simplify your workflow, save time, and open

doors to new opportunities in building your online income.

- **Chapter 3: The AI Web Accelerator Framework—Your Key Strategy for Quick Results**
  Learn my proprietary framework for seamlessly integrating AI tools and strategies to achieve consistent growth and measurable outcomes.

- **Chapter 4: Leveraging AI for Massive Productivity Gains**
  Uncover strategies to automate repetitive tasks, streamline processes, and accomplish more in less time with AI-powered tools.

- **Chapter 5: Building a Powerful Online Brand Using AI**
  Learn how to leverage AI to create a strong online presence, build trust with your audience, and elevate your brand across digital platforms.

- **Chapter 6: Creating Wealth with AI-Generated Products**
  Discover how to create and market AI-generated products that can become scalable sources of revenue.

- **Chapter 7: Real-World Results—Case Studies and Success Stories**
  Dive into inspiring examples of businesses and individuals who have used these strategies to achieve incredible success.

- **Chapter 8: AI Isn't Perfect, But It's Close Enough**
  Understand the strengths and limitations of AI, and learn how to navigate its imperfections to achieve exceptional results.

- **Chapter 9: Navigating AI's Agreeability Bias—Avoiding the Echo Chamber Effect**
  Learn how to guide AI to provide balanced and accurate responses, avoiding common pitfalls like bias and overly agreeable outputs.

- **Chapter 10: Debunking AI Myths—Breaking Barriers to Embrace the Future**
  Dispel common misconceptions about AI, from fears of job loss to concerns about complexity, and discover why these myths shouldn't hold you back.

- **Chapter 11: The AI Entrepreneur's Toolkit—Tools for Success**
  Explore a curated list of AI tools tailored for

entrepreneurs, creators, and professionals, along with actionable strategies for using them effectively.

- **Chapter 12: The Future of AI—Staying Ahead of the Curve**
  Get a glimpse into emerging trends and innovations shaping the future of AI, and learn how to position yourself for long-term success in this exciting landscape.

Conclusion: Turning AI Tools into Lasting Success
We'll wrap up with guidance on how to integrate these tools into your long-term strategy for ongoing success and impact.

This journey is yours to take. If you're ready to unlock the potential of AI and web tools, I invite you to dive into this book with me. Together, we'll explore the systems, strategies, and tools that can help you achieve the goals you've always envisioned—no matter how big or ambitious they may be.

Are you ready to take that next step into the future? Are you ready to unlock the productivity producing potential that this new innovative technology has to offer? Then continue onto Chapter 1 as we get started on this amazing adventure together.

Chapter 1:
The AI Advantage – Why AI is The Future of Online Success

Imagine having a tool that could instantly amplify your productivity, help you engage with your audience more effectively, and free up hours in your day to focus on what truly matters.

That's the promise of artificial intelligence—an innovative technology that is rapidly transforming industries, reshaping businesses, and empowering individuals to achieve more than ever before.

But AI isn't just for large corporations or tech giants. Today, AI is accessible to everyone, including entrepreneurs, creators, and small business owners. With the right tools, anyone can harness AI to optimize their workflows, automate repetitive tasks, and even generate entirely new revenue streams.

The Game-Changing Potential of AI

At its core, AI is about making data-driven decisions, automating processes, and producing creative outputs at a scale and speed that would be impossible manually. For entrepreneurs and business owners, this means more than just efficiency—it's about creating impact. AI allows you to scale your efforts, reach more people, and deliver value faster than ever before.

For example, consider how AI can streamline content creation. Imagine having an AI assistant that can analyze a transcript of a podcast and create a summarized, search-optimized social media post. Or envision a tool that can help design your logo and branding materials without the need for a graphic designer. With AI, these processes are no longer bound by the limitations of time or human resources.

These possibilities aren't just theoretical; they're real and available to anyone willing to embrace AI as a fundamental part of their toolkit. But to truly unlock AI's potential, it's essential to understand why it's so powerful—and how to integrate it into your own strategies.

Why AI is a Must-Have for Modern Entrepreneurs

1. **AI Saves Time by Automating Repetitive Tasks**
   One of the greatest advantages of AI is its ability to handle time-consuming, repetitive tasks with precision and speed. For instance, social media scheduling, content creation, email marketing, and data analysis can all be streamlined through AI tools. By automating these tasks, you're not only saving time—

you're also freeing up mental energy for higher-impact activities.

2. **AI Enhances Decision-Making with Data-Driven Insights**
   Today's AI tools go beyond automation; they offer advanced analytics and insights that can drive your decision-making process. AI can analyze audience behavior, market trends, and competitor activities, giving you actionable insights to improve your strategies. This level of data analysis is invaluable for entrepreneurs who want to stay ahead and make informed choices.

3. **AI Expands Your Creative Capabilities**
   Many people associate AI with automation, but it's also a powerful tool for creativity. AI-driven design and content generation tools allow you to experiment with new ideas, produce original content, and maintain a consistent brand image—all without needing specialized skills. Whether you're creating graphics, videos, or written content, AI can enhance your creative output and elevate your brand's visual identity.

4. **AI Provides Scalability Without Additional Overhead**
   Traditionally, scaling a business meant

hiring more people, expanding operations, and increasing overhead costs. AI changes the equation by allowing you to scale your efforts without the need for additional staff. With AI tools handling much of the workload, you can grow your business, increase output, and serve more clients—all with minimal extra costs.

Why Now is the Best Time to Integrate AI into Your Business

AI has been a growing force in technology for years, but something remarkable is happening right now. We're at a unique moment in history where AI is more powerful, accessible, and affordable than ever before. Waiting to adopt AI isn't just delaying progress—it's risking being left behind in a rapidly evolving world.

The Convergence of Power and Accessibility

Just a decade ago, AI was confined to massive corporations with billion-dollar budgets and specialized teams of researchers. Today, that's no longer the case. The tools that once required advanced technical expertise are now at your fingertips, thanks to user-friendly interfaces and subscription-based models.

- **Accessibility**: Platforms like ChatGPT and Canva with AI are intuitive enough for anyone to use, whether you're a solopreneur or leading a team.
- **Affordability**: For as little as the cost of a monthly streaming subscription, you can access tools that rival what only the most advanced companies could afford a few years ago.

This democratization of AI means there's no longer a barrier between you and the game-changing potential of this technology.

An Accelerating Landscape

AI is evolving faster than any technology in history. Every month, new tools, updates, and breakthroughs are hitting the market. By adopting AI now, you position yourself to take full advantage of this momentum. You'll be ahead of the curve while others are still trying to figure out how to adapt.

- **Example**: Businesses using AI today are automating workflows, cutting costs, and generating content at speeds previously unthinkable. Those who hesitate risk playing catch-up in an increasingly AI-driven economy.

The Cost of Hesitation

While it's tempting to wait and see how AI develops, the cost of inaction can be steep. Consider this:

- Businesses that delay adopting AI risk falling behind competitors who embrace it.
- Creators and entrepreneurs who ignore AI tools may struggle to keep up with the efficiency and scalability of those who use them.

The longer you wait, the harder it becomes to bridge the gap. Adopting AI today means you're not just keeping pace—you're setting the pace.

Opportunities in the Now

This moment is particularly ripe for AI adoption because:

- **Tools Are Easier to Learn Than Ever**: Tutorials, guides, and community forums make onboarding quick and simple.

- **The Competition Isn't Fully Onboard Yet**: You have a window of opportunity to establish yourself as an early adopter in your industry.
- **AI Is Still a Differentiator**: Using AI today can help you stand out, whereas waiting may mean merely keeping up.

Taking Action

The question isn't whether you should adopt AI. It's *why wouldn't you start now?* By integrating AI into your business today, you're not just gaining tools—you're gaining a competitive edge that will position you for success in the years to come.

To illustrate how AI can give you an unfair advantage over your competition and transform your business, I'll share with you a quick personal business story.

Personal Story: Discovering AI's Advantage

A few years ago, I was juggling multiple projects, all demanding more time than I had to give. One particular project involved creating weekly blog content for a website I was managing. Normally, it would take me hours to research, outline, and write a single post, not to mention proofreading and optimizing it for search engines.

This, combined with the online API development we were doing for a client, the software development efforts involved in creating a website that generated eight- and nine-figure revenues for their company and organization, and the video productions my media company was handling, this all added up to a very hectic and stressful time.

I was overwhelmed, and honestly, I didn't think I could keep up. That's when I decided to test out an AI-powered writing tool I had heard about. I was skeptical at first, but within minutes, the tool analyzed my ideas, helped structure the content, and even suggested headlines and keywords. What would have taken me five hours was done in less than one.

The best part? The quality of the post wasn't just good—it was exceptional. I could tweak and refine the draft to fit my voice, but 80% of the heavy lifting was already done. With the time I saved, I was able to focus on higher-priority tasks, like developing my brand strategy and planning the next quarter's projects.

That was my lightbulb moment. I realized that AI wasn't just a tool—it was a productivity partner, one that could transform how I worked and help me achieve results I hadn't thought possible. And it didn't stop there. Over the following months, I began integrating more AI tools into my workflow, from social media management to visual design, and the impact was undeniable.

Tackling Common Misconceptions About AI

AI is rapidly transforming the way we work, create, and grow, yet some misconceptions hold people back from fully embracing its potential. Let's address three of the most common fears surrounding AI, break them down, and empower you with actionable steps to overcome them.

Later in this book, we'll dive deeper into these and other myths in Chapter 10, "Debunking AI Myths—Breaking Barriers to Embrace the Future." But for now, let's tackle three big concerns I hear all the time.

Let's address three of the most common fears about AI head-on, so you can move forward with clarity and confidence.

---

1. "AI Is Too Complex or Technical"

By now, you can see the incredible potential of AI to revolutionize your workflow and amplify your results. But as with any transformative technology, it's natural to have some hesitations.

I know you're probably thinking, *"This is easy for you, Steve. After all, you're a high-tech entrepreneur and business owner. You've been a software engineer for over 20 years and worked for the last 30 years in the high-tech space. But it's too complex and technical for me!"*

Let me stop you right there. Yes, I've been fortunate to work in the tech world for decades, but here's the truth: You don't need to be a tech guru to leverage AI. These tools are designed for *you*—the business owner, creator, or solopreneur who doesn't have time to learn coding or advanced programming.

In fact, it was our understanding some 30 years ago that our technology would eventually grow to a point where everyone could utilize these powerful tools to meet their needs, be it from business to artistic expression, to even computer programming itself. This way everyone could take advantage of this technology allowing their creativity, productivity, and innovation to flourish.

AI tools are becoming increasingly user-friendly. Many of them require no more than a simple prompt or click of a button.

Actionable Advice: Start Small

- **Choose One Tool**: Begin with an easy-to-use platform like ChatGPT or Canva. Use ChatGPT to write social media captions or Canva to design a logo. Both require no technical expertise.
- **Experiment Without Fear**: Don't worry about doing it perfectly—AI is all about iteration. Test prompts, play with designs, and see what works for you.
- **Use Tutorials**: Many tools include built-in guides or tutorials. Spend just 15 minutes exploring one to see how much you can accomplish.

The complexity of AI isn't a barrier—it's an illusion. With the right tools, you can harness the power of AI as effortlessly as sending an email.

---

2. "AI Will Replace Human Jobs Entirely"

One of the most widespread fears about AI is that it will completely replace human jobs, leaving us irrelevant. But let's set the record straight: AI isn't here to replace humanity—it's here to work alongside us, amplifying our creativity and efficiency.

Think about it. AI is trained on *human creativity*—art, words, photos, music, and more. It doesn't create in a vacuum; it builds upon the human experience. Without us, there is no AI.

Examples of Collaboration with AI:

- **Art and Design**: Tools like MidJourney or Leonardo AI don't eliminate artists—they give them superpowers. Imagine being able to test 20 design ideas in minutes, then refining the best one with your personal touch.
- **Writing and Content Creation**: AI can draft an article, but it's your insights, stories, and voice that turn it into something truly meaningful.

The Consequences of Not Adapting

While AI won't replace all jobs, it will impact those who refuse to adapt. If you're hesitant to embrace it, you risk being left behind as competitors who adopt AI gain speed, efficiency, and scalability.

Here's the reality: AI enhances your capabilities. It's not a threat to your creativity—it's a partner that helps you reach your full potential.

Actionable Advice: Embrace AI as a Co-Creator

- Start small with AI tools in your field—whether it's generating design mockups or brainstorming blog topics.
- Experiment with collaborative workflows, using AI to handle repetitive tasks while focusing on your unique expertise.

---

3. "AI Is Unaffordable for Small Businesses or Solopreneurs"

Another common misconception is that AI is expensive and only accessible to big corporations with massive budgets. This couldn't be further from the truth.

Today's AI tools are often **Software as a Service (SaaS)** platforms, meaning they operate on affordable monthly subscriptions. For as little as $10 to $50 per month, you can access professional-grade tools that automate your tasks, design your graphics, or even analyze your data.

Examples of Affordable AI Tools:

- **ChatGPT**: Offers free and low-cost plans for writing, brainstorming, and automating text-based tasks.
- **Canva**: For less than $15/month, you get access to professional design capabilities.
- **Buffer**: Manage and schedule social media posts for less than the cost of a takeout lunch.

AI isn't just affordable—it's an investment that pays for itself by saving you time, streamlining your efforts, and generating more revenue.

Actionable Advice: Get Started for Free

- Many tools offer free trials or freemium versions. Start with those to explore what works for your needs.
- Calculate the time you'll save with AI and think of it as an investment in your business's growth.

Breaking Barriers to AI Adoption

The truth about AI is that it's not too complex, it's not here to replace you, and it's absolutely within your budget. The real challenge isn't AI itself—it's overcoming the misconceptions that hold you back.

By starting small, viewing AI as a collaborator, and exploring affordable options, you'll unlock its potential to save time, enhance creativity, and scale your efforts.

Remember: The goal isn't perfection; it's progress. Embrace AI as the tool it is—a powerful ally on your journey to achieving more.

The Road Ahead—Integrating AI for Lasting Success

This book is more than just a guide to AI tools and strategies—it's your blueprint for leveraging the power of AI to transform your business, your productivity, and your future. AI isn't just another tool in the box; it's a game-changing partner that can amplify your capabilities, streamline your efforts, and open doors you didn't even know existed.

From saving hours in repetitive tasks to creating stunning, professional-grade content, the benefits of AI are vast. But this book goes beyond the *what*—it's about the *how*. You'll discover actionable frameworks, real-world examples, and step-by-step guidance to ensure AI becomes an integral part of your workflow, helping you achieve measurable results.

As you move through these chapters, you'll uncover:

- The essential tools that will form the backbone of your AI strategy.
- Proven techniques to maximize efficiency and creativity while minimizing costs.
- A mindset shift that positions you to harness AI not as a competitor, but as a collaborator.
- A framework designed to accelerate your income, influence, and impact online.

But here's the key takeaway: AI is only as powerful as the person wielding it. This book will empower you with the confidence, clarity, and skills to wield AI effectively—not just to keep pace, but to lead in your field.

In the next chapter, we'll dive into the specific tools that will help you unlock AI's potential. These tools aren't just for tech experts—they're designed to be accessible, intuitive, and transformational for entrepreneurs, creators, and professionals alike. By the end of this journey, you'll have everything you need to thrive in the AI-powered future.

Chapter 2:
Web-Based Tools for Wealth - Essential AI Tools You Need

If you could have a toolbox full of powerful, easy-to-use tools that amplify your productivity and streamline your work, wouldn't you want to know exactly what's inside? That's what this chapter is all about: uncovering the essential AI tools that can help you create wealth, save time, and boost productivity—all without requiring advanced technical skills.

Today's AI tools are more accessible than ever, and the best part? Most of them are web-based, meaning you can access them from anywhere with an internet connection. Whether you're a solo entrepreneur, a small business owner, or someone looking to grow a side hustle, the right tools can turn your goals into tangible results.

The Criteria for Must-Have AI Tools

Before we dive into the list, let's establish some ground rules for what makes a tool "essential." The tools we'll cover in this chapter meet at least one (or several) of these criteria:

1. **Ease of Use**: You shouldn't need to be a tech expert to benefit from these tools. They're designed to be intuitive and user-friendly.
2. **Impact on Productivity**: The tool should save you significant time or reduce effort in your workflow.
3. **Versatility**: Ideally, it can be applied across multiple areas of your business or creative projects.
4. **Cost-Effectiveness**: These tools provide exceptional value for the price, with many offering free or affordable tiers.
5. **Proven Results**: They've been tested and validated by entrepreneurs, creators, or businesses to deliver measurable outcomes.

With these criteria in mind, let's explore the tools that can transform your workflow and drive your success.

The Essential AI Tools for Wealth and Productivity

"The fastest path to wealth isn't just working harder—it's working smarter."

1. AI for Content Creation and Marketing

One of the most time-intensive aspects of running a business is generating content. Whether it's blogs, social media posts, or email campaigns, AI tools can handle the heavy lifting.

- *What It Does*: These tools can analyze data, draft posts, and even suggest engaging headlines and copy tailored to your audience.
- *Use Case*: Imagine uploading a podcast transcript and receiving a search-optimized blog post or social media snippet within minutes.

2. AI for Visual Design and Branding

Consistent branding is key to building trust and recognition online, but not everyone has the resources for a full-time graphic designer. AI-powered tools can help you create stunning visuals.

- *What It Does*: These tools can generate logos, banners, and other design assets customized to your style and vision.
- *Use Case*: With just a few clicks, you can create polished marketing materials for your brand without waiting on a designer.

3. AI for Social Media Automation

Managing social media can be overwhelming, especially when you're trying to stay active on multiple platforms. AI can automate posting, engagement, and analytics, helping you stay consistent without the stress.

- *What It Does*: These tools schedule posts, suggest optimal posting times, and even help you track engagement.
- *Use Case*: Maintain an active online presence while freeing up hours every week.

4. AI for Video and Audio Editing

Video is one of the most powerful ways to connect with an audience, but editing can be tedious and time-consuming. AI tools streamline this process.

- *What It Does*: They can auto-generate captions, enhance audio quality, and even suggest edits to improve viewer engagement.
- *Use Case*: Produce professional-quality videos and podcasts in less time.

5. AI for Data Analysis and Decision-Making

Every business generates data, but making sense of it can be daunting. AI tools can help you uncover actionable insights without drowning in spreadsheets.

- *What It Does*: These tools analyze trends, predict outcomes, and provide recommendations to help you make smarter business decisions.

- *Use Case*: Quickly identify what's working in your strategy and where you should focus your efforts.

How to Choose the Right Tools for Your Goals

With so many tools available, it's important to choose ones that align with your specific needs. Ask yourself:

- **What's my biggest time sink?** Focus on tools that can automate or simplify those tasks.
- **What's my primary goal?** Whether it's building a brand, saving time, or increasing revenue, let your objectives guide your selection.
- **Do I need an all-in-one solution or specialized tools?** Some tools offer broad capabilities, while others excel in specific areas.

My Recommended AI Tools for Success

Each tool in this list has been carefully selected because it's helped me achieve remarkable results in my business. These tools have saved me time, enhanced my productivity, and opened new doors for creativity and impact. Below, I'll share why I recommend each tool and how it's made a difference in my workflow.

---

1. LLM Chat Models and Language Tools

These tools leverage advanced language models to help you generate content, brainstorm ideas, and tackle complex tasks with ease.

- **ChatGPT (OpenAI)** – *"This is my go-to tool for writing long-form content like blogs, marketing emails, and even detailed project outlines. It has helped me cut my content creation time in half, allowing me to focus on strategy instead of drafting."*
- **Gemini (Google DeepMind)** – *"Gemini excels at combining conversational fluency with factual precision. It's been a valuable tool for creating technical documentation and clear explanations for my courses."*
- **Claude (Anthropic)** – *"When I need research or a concise summary of a complex topic, Claude delivers spot-on results. It's like having a research assistant on demand."*

2. Image Generation Models

Create stunning visuals without needing a professional designer, perfect for branding, marketing, and creative projects.

- **MidJourney** – *"This tool has been invaluable for creating high-quality, artistic visuals for my branding and marketing campaigns. The level of detail it produces is unmatched."*
- **Leonardo AI** – *"When I need customizable image styles for projects like logos or banners, Leonardo AI provides the flexibility and precision I need."*
- **Canva (with AI)** – *"Canva's AI-powered templates are perfect for designing polished social media posts and marketing materials. It's intuitive and quick, making it a staple in my workflow."*
- **DALL-E (OpenAI)** – *"DALL-E shines in generating creative and photorealistic visuals, especially for unique design concepts I can't find elsewhere."*

3. Video Generation and Editing

Streamline video creation and editing with these tools that save time and boost production quality.

- **Pictory** – *"I use Pictory to quickly turn text scripts into professional-quality videos. It's perfect for creating explainer videos and course content."*
- **Leonardo AI** – *"Leonardo AI doubles as a great tool for generating visual assets for video projects, blending seamlessly into my video creation workflow."*
- **Runway ML** – *"Runway ML has been a game-changer for enhancing video quality with tools like object removal and AI-assisted editing. It's saved me countless hours."*
- **DeScript** – *"This all-in-one tool makes editing videos and podcasts effortless. Its auto-captioning and transcription features are particularly useful for repurposing content."*

---

4. AI Productivity Tools

Boost your efficiency and stay organized with tools designed to simplify and automate your workflows.

- **Notion AI** – *"Notion's AI capabilities help me brainstorm ideas, organize projects, and even draft content directly in my workspace. It's been a productivity powerhouse for me."*
- **Zapier** – *"This tool connects all my apps and automates repetitive tasks, freeing up hours every week for more strategic work."*
- **Trello (with AI-Powered Butler)** – *"Trello's AI-powered features make task management a breeze by automating reminders and prioritizing tasks based on deadlines."*

---

5. AI Tools for Social Media Posting and Scheduling

Stay consistent and engaging on social media with these tools that handle posting, analytics, and strategy.

- **Buffer** – *"Buffer helps me schedule posts across platforms and find the best times to engage with my audience. It's simple but incredibly effective."*
- **Hootsuite** – *"Hootsuite provides detailed analytics that help me refine my social media*

strategies. It's been instrumental in growing my brand presence."

- **ChatGPT (OpenAI)** – *"I use ChatGPT to draft engaging captions and generate fresh content ideas for social media posts, keeping my profiles active without the stress."*

---

6. AI Tools for Podcasting and Audio Cleanup

Enhance your audio quality and streamline podcast production with these powerful tools.

- **Adobe Podcast (Enhance)** – *"This tool dramatically improves audio quality by removing background noise and sharpening voices, making my podcasts sound professional with minimal effort."*
- **DeScript** – *"DeScript is my go-to for editing podcast episodes, from cutting silences to polishing audio levels. It's a must-have for any podcaster."*

---

7. AI Tools for Transcript Processing

Turn spoken content into actionable insights with tools that transcribe and process audio with accuracy.

- **Otter.ai** – *"Otter.ai makes it easy to transcribe meetings and interviews with high accuracy, saving me hours on manual transcription."*
- **Rev** – *"For critical projects, Rev combines AI automation with human review, ensuring near-perfect transcripts every time."*

How to Use These Tools

Each tool listed here is a stepping stone to greater productivity and success. But the real magic happens when you combine them into a cohesive strategy.

The strategy in many cases comes down to a strategic integration session which includes company wide adoption and training for your company or organization.

Why These Tools Matter

These tools aren't just about saving time—they're about creating opportunities. As I stated earlier, the fastest path to wealth isn't just working harder—it's working smarter. These tools can help you reclaim time, reduce costs, and focus on the activities that are important to your bottom line and strategic impact.

By freeing up your schedule and enhancing your capabilities, they give you the bandwidth to focus on high-impact activities. Whether it's scaling your business, building a brand, or exploring new income streams, the right tools can make all the difference.

In the next chapter, we'll go beyond tools and introduce a proprietary framework that ties everything together. This framework will show you how to integrate these tools into a cohesive strategy for maximum impact.

Chapter 3: The AI Web Accelerator Framework – Move Fast Strategy

What if you could accelerate your online success with a proven system that ties together all the key elements of digital growth?

Imagine your website as the central hub, similar to the city of your online presence, with a network of "streets" connecting traffic sources and engagement strategies directly back to it. This concept is the foundation of the AI Web Accelerator Framework, a simple yet powerful method to drive income, impact, and influence online.

Now, picture this: You launch your next big idea, and within days, your website traffic grows exponentially. Leads flow in from a coordinated network of social media, videos, and email campaigns—all tied together by a central strategy that practically runs itself. This isn't a fantasy; it's what the AI Web Accelerator Framework makes possible.

In this chapter, I'll introduce the MOVE FAST part of the framework, two core components of this system. Together, they provide a roadmap for leveraging AI and web tools to quickly build traffic, enhance engagement, and grow your brand. It will teach you how to make a FAST MOVE in order to MOVE FAST in the online space.

While this chapter focuses on the high-level strategy, the full framework—revealed in my course—dives deeper into managing and scaling your efforts across multiple touchpoints. I'll share that as well later I this chapter.

The Origins of the Framework

When I first developed this framework, I was overwhelmed by the fragmented nature of online marketing. I was juggling social media platforms, ad campaigns, and email strategies, all while trying to grow my own brand. It felt like running in a dozen directions at once—none of them fast enough to make significant progress.

One day, while brainstorming ways to simplify my efforts, I thought, *What if I treated my website like the central city, a central hub, with all my strategies being the streets connecting back to it?* That single insight was the turning point. By organizing my outreach, video efforts, and email campaigns into a cohesive system, I finally saw consistent growth.

For instance, I applied the framework to a side project—a niche blog I had struggled to grow. Using MOVE to focus on targeted outreach and FAST to optimize the sales funnel, I doubled website traffic and increased sign-ups for my lead magnet within three months. That's when I realized: This framework wasn't just a tool—it was the solution I had been searching for.

The Power of Simplification: A Story of Transformation

Let me share another example of how this framework transformed someone's business. Meet Rebecca, a freelance designer who felt buried under the weight of managing multiple platforms. Her website was barely generating traffic, and her social media efforts were scattered at best. She knew she needed a better system but didn't have the time—or budget—for trial and error.

When Rebecca started using the MOVE framework, her first step was to focus on video content. With the help of AI tools, she created a series of short tutorials showcasing her expertise. Each video linked back to her website, where she offered a free guide to building better brand designs. By aligning her efforts with the FAST framework, Rebecca built a simple sales funnel that nurtured these leads into paying clients. Within six months, she landed three major projects and grew her income by 40%.

The key to Rebecca's success? She stopped trying to do everything at once and focused on the elements that would yield the highest returns. That's the power of the AI Web Accelerator Framework—it's designed to simplify your efforts while amplifying your results.

Why This Framework Matters Today

You might be wondering, Why is this framework so effective now? The answer lies in timing and technology. AI has democratized the tools we once thought were only available to big corporations. From automated content creation to advanced analytics, these tools allow even solopreneurs to build systems that scale like never before.

The AI Web Accelerator Framework isn't just about working smarter; it's about leveling the playing field. By focusing on key strategies that connect back to your central city—your central hub—your website—you can achieve results that once seemed out of reach.

What's Next?

In the next sections, we'll explore the MOVE and FAST parts of the framework and how they function inside a broader system I refer to as the AI Web Accelerator Framework.

In practice, MOVE and FAST represent two structural components within a larger model used to evaluate how organizations and professionals move from isolated experimentation into coherent, integrated systems of work.

The purpose of introducing them here is not to present a complete methodology, but to give you a working structure you can apply immediately, one that clarifies how momentum, alignment, and intelligent deployment begin to take shape.

Now, let's step into the MOVE and FAST frameworks. The pages ahead will walk through how these concepts can be applied in practice, so they move beyond ideas and begin shaping how work is actually done.

The MOVE Framework

Driving engagement and traffic through interconnected components.

At the heart of MOVE is the idea of focusing your efforts on key areas that generate traffic and engagement while tying everything back to your website as the central hub. Each component is essential for building momentum and creating a sustainable online presence.

M: Marketing

General outreach strategies (paid ads, organic SEO).

Marketing is the engine that drives awareness and visibility for your brand. Whether it's through paid advertising or organic search engine optimization (SEO), the goal is to bring people into your ecosystem.

- **Paid Ads**: AI-powered tools make creating and targeting ads easier than ever. Imagine running Facebook or Google ads with precise targeting to reach your ideal audience.
- **Organic SEO**: By optimizing your website's content with AI tools for keyword research and on-page improvements, you can attract consistent traffic without ongoing ad spend.

- *Example*: *"With just one AI-driven SEO audit, I identified high-potential keywords that doubled my website traffic in a month."*

O: Outreach

Social media platforms, collaborations, and partnerships.

Outreach is about extending your reach through connections—whether via collaborations, partnerships, or direct social media engagement. In the MOVE framework, focus on **one** key social media platform where your audience spends the most time.

- **Collaborations**: Partner with influencers or complementary businesses to expand your audience.
- **Social Media**: Choose a platform like Instagram or Facebook and consistently engage your audience with content, comments, and direct messages.
- *Example*: *"By narrowing my focus to one platform, I doubled my engagement rate in less time."*

V: Video

YouTube, short-form video content like Reels or TikToks.

Video is the most engaging form of content, and

platforms like YouTube, TikTok, and Instagram Reels reward consistency. Focus on creating short, impactful videos that align with your brand's message.

- **AI Tools for Video**: Use tools like Pictory or Runway ML to simplify editing and enhance video quality.
- *Example*: *"With AI-powered video tools, I reduced my video production time by 75% and saw a 40% increase in views."*

E: Email

Nurturing leads and driving traffic back to the hub. Email remains one of the most effective channels for converting visitors into loyal customers. By using AI tools to craft personalized email campaigns, you can nurture leads and guide them back to your website.

- **Email Automation**: Tools like Notion AI or Zapier can help you automate follow-ups and segment your audience for better targeting.
- *Example*: *"With automated email workflows, I re-engaged dormant leads and increased click-through rates by 25%."*

The FAST Framework

A sleek, actionable approach to traffic acceleration.

While MOVE focuses on building engagement, FAST is about creating and optimizing pathways to drive traffic more effectively. Think of it as the execution plan that accelerates your results.

F: Funnels

Building pathways to guide prospects to the website.
A well-designed funnel takes prospects on a journey—from discovering your brand to becoming loyal customers.

- **AI Tools for Funnels**: Use AI to craft landing pages, automate follow-ups, and analyze conversion rates.
- *Example*: *"An AI-optimized funnel helped me double my course sign-ups with minimal effort."*

AI: Artificial Intelligence

Leveraging the power of AI to create content and posts.
AI is the cornerstone of this framework, enabling you to create content faster and with greater impact.

- **Content Creation**: AI tools like ChatGPT and Writesonic can generate blogs, social media captions, and ad copy in minutes.
- *Example*: *"By using AI for content creation, I freed up 10 hours a week to focus on strategy."*

S: Social Media

Organic reach and engagement.

Social media is one of the fastest ways to grow your audience. The key is consistency and quality.

- **AI for Social Media**: Use tools like Buffer or Hootsuite to schedule posts and track analytics.
- *Example*: *"With AI-powered scheduling, I maintained a consistent posting schedule without spending hours online."*

T: Traffic Optimization

Tracking; SEO, analytics, and continual improvement.

Traffic optimization is about analyzing what's working and making data-driven adjustments.

- **AI Analytics Tools**: Use tools like Google Analytics or AI-powered dashboards to gain insights into user behavior.

- *Example*: *"By tracking my website's performance, I identified and fixed a key bottleneck, increasing conversions by 15%."*

Unlocking the Full Framework

The MOVE and FAST frameworks establish an entry point into a broader way of thinking about intelligent systems. As the book continues, the focus will shift from individual tactics toward how these elements combine into larger operational structures, feedback loops, and long-term positioning..

Chapter 4: Leveraging AI for Massive Productivity Gains

What if you could accomplish in one hour what used to take an entire day?

That's the power of AI when applied to productivity. By automating repetitive tasks, streamlining processes, and enhancing creativity, AI empowers you to work smarter, not harder.

Take Lisa, for example. She's a solopreneur juggling social media management, email campaigns, and customer inquiries. Her days felt like a never-ending to-do list, leaving no room for the strategic thinking her business needed to grow. Once she embraced AI, everything changed. Automating her social media posts and email follow-ups freed up hours each week, allowing her to focus on launching a new product line—and it became her best-selling item to date.

Now imagine Carlos, the owner of a small restaurant in a bustling downtown area. His challenges were different. Carlos needed to streamline his ordering process, manage online reviews, and stay connected with customers on social media—all while ensuring the restaurant operated smoothly during peak hours. It was overwhelming. After exploring AI solutions, he implemented a chatbot to handle online reservations and answer common questions like "Do you have gluten-free options?" or "What time does brunch start?" He also used AI analytics tools to track which menu items were performing best and make data-driven decisions on weekly specials. The result? A 20% increase in customer satisfaction scores and more time for Carlos to focus on enhancing the in-restaurant experience.

Then there's Jane, a project manager working in a mid-sized corporate office. She faced the constant pressure of meeting deadlines, coordinating between departments, and ensuring no detail slipped through the cracks. Jane discovered AI-powered scheduling and task management tools, which allowed her to streamline workflows and automate meeting reminders. She even used AI for drafting initial project reports, saving hours every week. A quick disclaimer here: if you work in a corporate setting like Jane, be sure to check with your workplace to ensure AI tools are approved. Once Jane demonstrated the ROI of these tools—showing her manager how they saved time and improved team coordination—they became an integral part of her department's operations.

In this chapter, I'll show you how to use AI tools to free up your time and focus on the activities that matter most—whether it's building your brand, developing new products, or increasing your income. These strategies will help you turn AI into your ultimate productivity partner.

The Evolution of Productivity Tools

"Remember when productivity meant jotting tasks on a sticky note or using a physical planner? Today, AI doesn't just organize your tasks—it learns your habits, predicts your needs, and optimizes your workflow in ways that weren't possible even a decade ago."

Productivity has always been a cornerstone of human achievement. From the moment early civilizations began tracking time with sundials to organizing activities with ledgers, humanity has sought ways to do more in less time. The tools we've used to stay productive have evolved significantly, mirroring advances in technology and societal needs.

The Early Days: Paper and Pen

For centuries, productivity revolved around handwritten tools—journals, notebooks, and planners. These tools helped individuals map out daily tasks, maintain schedules, and jot down reminders. While effective in their time, they lacked the ability to adapt or provide insights beyond what was manually written.

The Digital Revolution: Computers and Software

The advent of computers in the late 20th century transformed productivity. Software like Microsoft Excel and early task management tools allowed for greater organization and automation, albeit on a limited scale. Digital calendars replaced paper planners, and email became the centerpiece of workplace communication. These tools streamlined workflows but still required significant manual input.

The Internet Era: Connectivity and Collaboration

With the rise of the internet, productivity tools became more collaborative. Platforms like Trello and Asana enabled teams to manage projects remotely, breaking down barriers of location and time zones. Cloud-based services like Google Drive brought real-time collaboration to documents, making productivity a shared experience. However, even with these advances, users still needed to invest time in learning how to navigate and optimize these tools.

The AI Leap: A New Era of Productivity

Enter AI—the game-changer that doesn't just assist with productivity but actively enhances it. Unlike earlier tools that relied on manual inputs and static processes, AI-powered tools adapt to your habits, predict your needs, and automate repetitive tasks. They don't just help you work faster; they help you work smarter.

For example:

- **Scheduling**: Tools like Clockwise analyze your calendar and suggest the best times for deep work, ensuring you stay focused without interruptions.
- **Content Creation**: Platforms like ChatGPT generate ideas, drafts, and even polished articles in minutes, allowing you to scale your creative output.
- **Analytics**: AI-powered dashboards consolidate data and provide actionable insights, so you can focus on making informed decisions rather than sifting through spreadsheets.

A Personal Story: Witnessing the Evolution

When I began my career, productivity tools were limited to task lists and spreadsheets. I remember spending hours updating status reports and manually coordinating schedules with colleagues. Then, tools like Google Calendar and project management software came along, and suddenly, collaboration became easier. But it wasn't until I integrated AI into my workflow that I saw the real transformation.

For instance, using AI scheduling tools reduced the back-and-forth emails required to set up meetings, saving hours every week. Content creation tools allowed me to produce high-quality blog posts in a fraction of the time, freeing up mental energy for strategic thinking. Most recently, tools that can monitor and take notes during meetings—with permissions, of course—have been a game-changer, saving my team and me the time spent on note-taking. These tools not only transcribe what was said but also summarize key points, highlight takeaways, and generate actionable follow-ups. These shifts weren't just incremental—they were exponential, allowing me to achieve results that would have been impossible with traditional tools.

The Takeaway: Why the Evolution Matters

Understanding the evolution of productivity tools underscores one key insight: the tools you use define the results you achieve. Each leap—from paper to digital, from digital to cloud-based, and now to AI—has provided opportunities to do more with less. But unlike previous eras, AI represents not just a tool but a partner in productivity. It learns, adapts, and grows with you, turning the impossible into the achievable.

As you explore AI-powered tools in this book, remember that embracing these technologies is not just about keeping up—it's about staying ahead. The journey from sticky notes to AI dashboards is one of empowerment, and with AI, the best is yet to come.

The 3 Pillars of AI-Driven Productivity

---

1. Automation: Let AI Handle the Repetitive Work

Automation is one of the biggest advantages of AI. Tasks that once took hours can now be completed in minutes, leaving you free to focus on strategic priorities.

- **Examples**:
    - Social media scheduling with tools like Buffer or Hootsuite.
    - Email automation using AI-powered platforms like Zapier or Notion AI.
    - Data entry and organization with tools like Trello's AI Butler.

How It Helped Me:
"When I first started using AI for automation, I realized how much time I had been wasting on repetitive tasks. For example, setting up automated email follow-ups saved me three hours a week, allowing me to focus on creating new content and expanding my business."

Story: The Freelancer's Transformation
Take Emily, a freelance copywriter drowning in client deadlines. She was spending hours manually scheduling blog posts and emailing updates to clients. After implementing Zapier and Buffer, she not only saved 10 hours a week but also impressed her clients with timely, consistent updates. The automation made her look like a team of five when it was just her—and her revenue doubled within six months.

---

2. Content Creation: Get More Done in Less Time

AI tools can help you generate high-quality content faster than ever. From blog posts to social media captions, these tools simplify the creative process without sacrificing quality.

- **Examples**:

    - ChatGPT for writing blog posts, captions, and ad copy.
    - Writesonic for creating marketing materials.
    - Canva with AI for designing graphics and visuals.

Pro Tip:
"AI isn't a replacement for your unique voice—it's a tool to amplify it. Start with an AI-generated draft, then refine it to match your style and message."

How It Helped Me:
"When I first integrated AI into my content creation process, I was skeptical. Could it really match my tone and creativity? What I found was that AI gave me a solid first draft, saving hours of brainstorming. It allowed me to focus on refining and perfecting the content, making it uniquely mine."

---

3. Decision-Making: Use AI to Gain Insights and Optimize

AI tools don't just save time—they also help you make smarter decisions. By analyzing data and providing actionable insights, they enable you to optimize your strategies and focus on what works.

- **Examples**:

- Google Analytics for tracking website performance.
- Social media analytics in Hootsuite for audience engagement metrics.
- AI-powered dashboards for revenue and sales tracking.

How It Helped Me:
"Using AI to analyze my website traffic showed me which pages were driving the most conversions. By focusing my efforts there, I increased sales by 20% in just one month."

A Quick Win:
Imagine running a campaign and wondering why engagement is dropping. AI analytics tools can pinpoint exactly where users are dropping off and suggest solutions. That kind of insight turns guesswork into results-driven action.

Putting AI to Work in Your Day-to-Day

Here's how to make AI part of your daily workflow:

1. **Identify Your Time Drains**
   List three tasks that take up the most time in your week.

   - *Examples: Writing emails, managing social media, analyzing data.*

2. **Find the Right AI Tools**
   Match each task with an AI tool designed to streamline it.

   - *Writing emails → Zapier for automation.*
   - *Managing social media → Buffer or Hootsuite.*
   - *Analyzing data → Google Analytics or AI-powered dashboards.*

3. **Test and Adjust**
   Start small by automating one task and gradually incorporate more tools as you become comfortable.

Overcoming Resistance to AI in Productivity

Many people hesitate to embrace AI in their workflows. The reasons are varied, fear of losing the "human touch," doubts about effectiveness, or a lack of time to learn new tools. These concerns are valid but often rooted in misconceptions.

"Many people hesitate to integrate AI into their workflows because they fear it might strip away the human touch. However, AI is not about replacing creativity, it's about empowering it. By handling mundane tasks, AI gives you more time to focus on the big-picture ideas that make your work unique."

Addressing the Fear of Losing the Human Touch

One of the most common objections to using AI is the fear that it will replace creativity and personal connection. However, the reality is quite the opposite. AI enhances the creative process by taking care of repetitive or low-impact tasks, freeing you to focus on innovation and strategy.

- **Example**: A graphic designer worried that AI-generated visuals might diminish the uniqueness of their work. But by using tools like Canva's AI assistant to handle basic layouts and templates, they had more time to focus on designing custom illustrations that delighted their clients.

- **Pro Tip**: Think of AI as a collaborator rather than a replacement. It's like having an assistant who handles the groundwork, so you can focus on the masterpiece.

Conquering the Learning Curve

Another common barrier is the belief that integrating AI will require extensive training or disrupt existing workflows. While it's true that some tools have a learning curve, many AI solutions are designed to be user-friendly and intuitive.

- **Example**: When Jane, a small business owner, first heard about AI tools, she was skeptical. "I barely have time to manage my email," she thought, "how will I learn this?" But after a colleague recommended ChatGPT for generating email templates, she gave it a try. Within minutes, Jane had a polished, professional email ready to send to her clients. "It was easier than I expected," she admitted.

- **Pro Tip**: Start small. Pick one area of your workflow—like email or social media—and introduce an AI tool to handle just that. As you see results, you'll gain confidence to expand AI's role in your productivity.

The Time Investment Myth

Many people claim they're too busy to learn AI, not realizing that the small time investment pays off exponentially in saved hours and increased efficiency.

- **Example**: David, a restaurant owner, thought AI wasn't relevant to his industry. However, when he started using an AI-powered scheduling tool for his staff, he saved three hours a week that he used to spend manually creating shifts. "I never thought a tool like this could make such a difference," David said. "Now I can focus on customer satisfaction instead of admin tasks."
- **Pro Tip**: Schedule a 30-minute "exploration session" to test an AI tool relevant to your needs. View it as an investment, not a disruption.

Shifting the Mindset

Embracing AI requires a mindset shift. Instead of seeing AI as a disruptor, view it as an enabler—a tool that helps you focus on high-value activities while automating the mundane.

- **Actionable Takeaway**: Write down three tasks you do regularly that are repetitive or time-consuming. Research an AI tool that can handle one of these tasks, and test it for a week. Note the time saved and consider how to reinvest that time into strategic work.

Why Overcoming Resistance Matters

Overcoming resistance to AI is not just about improving productivity—it's about staying competitive in an ever-evolving world. The choice isn't whether to use AI but how to use it effectively. By addressing these fears and barriers head-on, you can unlock the true potential of AI to transform your work and your business.

Case Study: My AI Productivity Breakthrough

"A year ago, I was overwhelmed by the sheer volume of tasks on my plate—managing social media, creating content, and analyzing metrics. I decided to integrate AI into my workflow, starting with social media scheduling and email automation. The results were incredible. Not only did I save over 10 hours a week, but I also saw a 30% increase in engagement on my posts and a 25% boost in email click-through rates. AI didn't just make me more productive—it made my efforts more effective."

Boosting Productivity: The Five Key Components and How AI Supercharges Them

When it comes to achieving maximum productivity, there are universal principles that hold true regardless of the tools you use. Whether you're managing a business, growing your brand, or simply trying to optimize your day-to-day tasks, mastering these five key components of productivity is essential. But here's the game-changer: AI doesn't just support these fundamentals—it enhances and accelerates them, making it easier than ever to achieve your goals.

---

1. Clarity and Prioritization

Defining clear goals and prioritizing tasks to align with those goals. Tools like to-do lists, Kanban boards, or Eisenhower matrices are often used for this.

- **How AI Helps**:
  AI-powered tools like Notion AI and Trello's AI Butler bring prioritization to a new level. These tools can automatically sort tasks based on urgency, suggest deadlines, and even group similar tasks for better focus. AI can also analyze your work patterns to identify which goals need more immediate attention.
- **Example**:
  "When I started using Notion AI, it suggested restructuring my task list to prioritize client deadlines over internal projects. That simple shift helped me avoid a major bottleneck and deliver on time."

---

2. Time Management

Effectively allocating time for tasks through techniques like time blocking, Pomodoro, or batching similar tasks together.

- **How AI Helps**:
  AI tools like Clockwise and Motion use advanced algorithms to schedule your day. They can integrate with your calendar to identify open blocks of time, suggest

optimized schedules, and even automate reminders for focused work sessions.

- **Example**:
  "Using Clockwise, I adopted time-blocking effortlessly. It automatically scheduled uninterrupted work blocks for my most critical tasks, increasing my focus and productivity by 30%."

---

3. Focus and Minimization of Distractions

Maintaining a focused mindset by reducing interruptions, avoiding multitasking, and creating an environment conducive to deep work.

- **How AI Helps**:
  AI can create distraction-free workspaces by silencing notifications, scheduling breaks, and even suggesting mindfulness practices. Tools like Serene and RescueTime track your digital activity, identifying patterns of distraction and providing actionable insights to minimize them.

- **Example**:
  "When I started using RescueTime, it flagged how much time I was spending on email during deep work hours. By scheduling email checks through AI-powered reminders, I

reduced interruptions and completed projects faster."

---

4. Energy Management

Balancing physical and mental energy by ensuring adequate sleep, nutrition, exercise, and breaks throughout the day.

- **How AI Helps**:
  AI-powered wellness apps like Headspace or MyFitnessPal can recommend meditation routines, track hydration, and suggest meal plans tailored to your energy needs. Some tools even integrate with wearable devices to monitor stress levels and provide personalized tips to recharge effectively.
- **Example**:
  "Using an AI-integrated fitness tracker, I realized that mid-afternoon walks boosted my energy levels significantly. This small change kept me refreshed and productive during long workdays."

---

5. Consistency and Habits

Building daily habits that support productivity, such as a morning routine, structured planning sessions, or continuous self-improvement practices.

- **How AI Helps**:
  Habit-tracking apps like Streaks and Habitica leverage AI to keep you accountable. These tools provide reminders, track progress, and even gamify your habits to make staying consistent fun and rewarding.
- **Example**:
  "With Streaks, I built a habit of starting each day with a 10-minute planning session. The app's reminders and streak tracker motivated me to stick with it, and my productivity skyrocketed."

AI as Your Productivity Coach

When you combine these five pillars with the power of AI, productivity becomes less about working harder and more about working smarter. AI doesn't just help you manage tasks—it empowers you to approach them strategically, ensuring your time and energy are spent where they matter most.

By integrating these principles and tools into your daily routine, you can create a productivity system that's not only effective but also sustainable. AI makes this easier than ever, freeing you to focus on what truly drives your business and personal growth.

The AI Mindset: Think Like a Time Hacker

Using AI isn't just about the tools—it's about adopting a mindset that prioritizes efficiency and impact.

- **Eliminate**: Identify tasks that no longer need your attention and delegate them to AI.
- **Automate**: Look for repetitive processes that can be streamlined.
- **Elevate**: Use the time saved to focus on high-impact activities like strategy, networking, and innovation.

The Consultant Who Mastered AI

John, a business consultant, was drowning in back-office tasks. By applying the "Eliminate, Automate, Elevate" method, he automated his invoicing process, eliminated manual data entry, and used the saved hours to pitch a new service offering. The result? A 35% revenue increase in just one quarter.

Debunking the "Too Busy to Learn AI" Myth

"It's easy to feel like there's no time to learn something new, but integrating AI into your workflow doesn't have to be overwhelming. Many tools are designed to be intuitive and can save you hours for every few minutes you invest in learning."

This sentiment resonates with so many entrepreneurs, professionals, and creators. The demands of a busy schedule can make any new initiative feel like a luxury you can't afford. But here's the paradox: by not investing in AI, you're likely working harder—not smarter.

Think about it: How much time do you spend on repetitive tasks, searching for solutions, or creating content from scratch? Imagine reclaiming those hours each week and redirecting them toward the projects and goals that truly matter to you. AI offers that opportunity, but only if you're willing to take the first step.

The ROI of Learning AI

Learning AI doesn't require a full-time commitment. Many tools are designed with simplicity in mind, allowing you to integrate them into your workflow without needing a technical background. For instance:

- **Social Media Automation**: Spending 30 minutes learning how to use a tool like Buffer can save you hours each month by scheduling posts in advance.
- **Content Creation**: Tools like ChatGPT can turn your ideas into polished blog posts, freeing up time for strategy or other high-impact activities.
- **Data Analysis**: Platforms like Google Analytics offer intuitive dashboards that provide actionable insights at a glance, eliminating the need to comb through endless spreadsheets.

Each minute spent learning these tools can save hours—or even days—down the line.

A Story of Realization

Take Anna, a small business owner running a boutique fitness studio. Between teaching classes, managing memberships, and handling marketing, she barely had a moment to breathe. "I don't have time to learn AI," she told herself repeatedly. But after her assistant left for a new opportunity, Anna had no choice but to explore automation. In less than an hour, she set up an AI-powered chatbot to handle customer inquiries. To her surprise, not only did she save three hours a week, but her clients also appreciated the instant responses.

The experience was a revelation. "I thought I was too busy for AI, but AI made me less busy."

Shifting the Mindset

Adopting AI isn't about adding more to your plate—it's about clearing it. Think of it this way: AI is an investment in your future efficiency. The initial time spent learning these tools pays dividends in time saved, stress reduced, and results achieved.

Here's a simple challenge: Choose one task you find particularly draining—whether it's managing emails, creating social media content, or scheduling meetings. Research an AI tool designed for that specific need and commit to testing it for a week. The time saved will speak for itself.

Looking Ahead

AI can transform your productivity, but it's only part of the equation. In the next chapter, we'll explore how to use AI tools to build and amplify your online brand—helping you create a presence that resonates with your audience and drives long-term success.

Chapter 5: Building a Powerful Online Brand Using AI

Your online brand is your digital handshake. It's how your audience connects with you, decides if they trust you, and ultimately chooses to engage. But building a brand can feel like an overwhelming maze of social media posts, content creation, and endless decisions about where to focus your energy.

That's where AI becomes a game-changer. With the right tools and strategies, AI simplifies the process, helping you build a professional, engaging, and memorable brand—without the stress or the steep learning curve.

In this chapter, I'll show you how AI tools can help you:

1. Refine your message to resonate with your audience.
2. Build genuine connections without sacrificing your time.
3. Unlock creativity to make your brand visually unforgettable.

We'll start with the three pillars of a strong online brand: **Clarity, Connection, and Creativity.**

The Foundations of a Powerful Online Brand

A successful online brand isn't just about flashy visuals or witty social media posts—it's about creating a cohesive experience that draws your audience in. At its core, every strong brand stands on these three pillars:

strong online brand has three key components:

1. **Clarity**: Your audience should instantly understand who you are, what you do, and why they should care. Your brand's message and identity should be consistent across platforms.

2. **Connection**: Authentic engagement builds trust, turning one-time visitors into lifelong fans. Build meaningful relationships with your audience through authentic engagement.

3. **Creativity**: Stand out with unique, eye-catching content that reflects your brand's personality, and makes you memorable in a crowded digital world.

AI can support all three areas, making it easier than ever to grow your brand effectively. To bring this to life, let's explore a real-world example of how these principles work together.

To illustrate these pillars in action, let me tell you about Sara.

A Story of Transformation: *How Sara Built Her Brand from Scratch*

Sara was a fitness coach who dreamed of launching her own online business. She had the expertise and passion but no clue how to build her brand. "I'm not tech-savvy," she confessed to me during our first call. "How can I compete with people who have professional designers and social media teams?"

We began with **Clarity**. Using ChatGPT, Sara crafted her brand mission: *"Helping busy moms build strength and confidence in just 30 minutes a day."* This simple, compelling statement became the foundation of her messaging across all platforms.

Next, we tackled **Connection**. Instead of spreading herself thin across multiple platforms, Sara focused solely on Facebook, where her target audience—busy moms—spends time. Using ManyChat, she set up a chatbot to answer FAQs and share free workout tips. Her audience loved the instant responses, and her follower count grew steadily.

Finally, we turned to **Creativity**. Using Canva with AI, Sara designed a polished logo, social media banners, and a downloadable meal plan. Despite having no design experience, she created content that looked professional and on-brand.

In six months, Sara went from feeling overwhelmed to running a thriving online brand. Her secret? Focusing on one platform, leveraging AI, and staying consistent.

How AI Enhances Brand Clarity

Clarity is the cornerstone of a strong brand. It is the foundation of every strong brand. Without it, your audience won't know who you are or why they should care. It ensures that your audience knows what you offer, why it matters, and how it benefits them.

AI tools make it easier than ever to clarify your message and ensure it resonates. Here's how.

1. Designing Your Brand Voice

Your voice is the personality of your brand. Whether you want to sound professional, fun, or empathetic, tools like ChatGPT can help you define and refine your tone.

- **Example**: When crafting a tagline, Sara asked ChatGPT for variations that matched her mission, such as *"Strong Moms, Stronger Lives."* After testing a few options, she landed on the one that resonated most with her audience.

- **Pro Tip**: *Ask ChatGPT for variations in tone (e.g., casual, professional, humorous) to find the perfect fit for your brand.*

2. Designing a Consistent Visual Identity

Your visual branding—logos, colors, and typography—should be instantly recognizable. Tools like Canva with AI and MidJourney make it easy to create professional visuals without a design background.

- **Example**: Canva's templates can help you design cohesive social media posts, website banners, and presentations in minutes.

- **Pro Tip**: *Use MidJourney to generate unique, artistic designs that make your brand stand out from competitors.*

3. Streamlining Messaging Across Platforms

AI-powered content generators can help ensure your messaging is consistent across all platforms. From emails to Instagram captions, these tools save time while maintaining clarity.

- **Example**: Writesonic can draft content for different platforms, adapting the tone and style to fit each audience.

4. Polishing Visual Identity

Your visuals should be as recognizable as your voice. Canva with AI and MidJourney make designing logos, banners, and graphics effortless.

- **Example**: "Using Canva, I created a logo and social media graphics that felt cohesive and professional, giving my brand the polished look it needed to stand out."

5. Logos and Guides

Your audience should immediately understand who you are, what you offer, and why they should trust you. AI tools help ensure that your brand messaging is clear and consistent.

- **Logo and Branding Design**: Tools like Canva with AI and MidJourney can generate professional-quality logos and visuals in minutes.

    - *Example*: *"With Canva's AI templates, I was able to design a cohesive set of social media graphics, banners, and logos, giving my brand a polished, professional look."*

- **Content Style Guides**: Use tools like ChatGPT to create brand voice guidelines, ensuring your content stays aligned with your core values.
    - *Example*: *"By defining my brand voice with AI, I ensured that every post, email, and ad reflected the tone and personality I wanted my audience to experience."*

How AI Strengthens Brand Connection

Connection is what turns one-time visitors into loyal followers. Here's how AI tools can help you engage authentically and consistently.

1. Personalized Engagement

AI tools like ManyChat allow you to set up chatbots that provide instant, personalized responses to customer inquiries. This keeps your audience engaged even when you're not available.

- **Example**: Set up an AI chatbot to handle FAQs, freeing up your time for more strategic tasks.
- **Pro Tip**: *Use ChatGPT to script responses that feel natural and conversational.*

2. Scheduling and Managing Social Media Content

Staying consistent on social media is essential for building trust. Tools like Buffer and Hootsuite can automate posting schedules, analyze engagement, and suggest optimal posting times.

- **Example**: Buffer's analytics can show which types of content perform best, helping you refine your strategy over time.
- **Pro Tip**: *Focus on one platform first—such as a Facebook Page—before expanding to others.*

3. Leveraging AI Analytics for Deeper Insights

AI-powered analytics tools provide valuable insights into audience behavior, enabling you to tailor your content and campaigns.

- **Example**: Hootsuite's analytics feature can track audience engagement metrics, such as likes, shares, and comments, to identify trends.

- **Pro Tip**: *Look for patterns in engagement to determine what resonates most with your audience.*

Authentic engagement is the heart of any successful brand. AI helps you stay connected with your audience by making interaction easier and more impactful.

- **Personalized Social Media Content**: AI tools like Writesonic and ChatGPT can create engaging captions tailored to your audience's interests.
    - *Example*: *"With AI-generated content ideas, I was able to maintain a consistent posting schedule on Instagram, which boosted my follower engagement by 40%."*
- **Customer Interaction Automation**: Use tools like ManyChat or ChatGPT to create AI-powered chatbots that provide instant responses to common customer inquiries.
    - *Example*: *"Setting up a chatbot on my Facebook Page allowed me to respond to customer questions 24/7, improving satisfaction and freeing up my time for strategy."*

How AI Boosts Brand Creativity

Creativity is the spark that makes your brand memorable. AI tools empower you to explore new ideas, test concepts, and produce high-quality content faster than ever.

- **Video Creation**: Tools like Pictory and Runway ML simplify video production, making it easy to create professional-looking videos without a large budget.
    - *Example*: *"I created a series of short videos for Instagram Reels using Pictory, which not only saved time but also increased my reach to a younger audience."*
- **Image Generation**: MidJourney and Leonardo AI allow you to design unique visuals that stand out in a crowded feed.
    - *Example*: *"Using AI-generated visuals, I was able to launch a campaign that attracted 20% more engagement than my previous efforts."*

Building Your Brand with AI: A Step-by-Step Guide

1. **Define Your Brand Identity**: Use AI tools to refine your mission, vision, and tone.
   - Tools: ChatGPT, Writesonic.
   - Action Step: Generate a list of brand values and create a style guide for your content.
2. **Optimize Your Visual Identity**: Design logos, banners, and graphics that reflect your brand's personality.
   - Tools: Canva with AI, MidJourney.
   - Action Step: Create a logo and set of branded templates for consistent visuals across platforms.
3. **Plan and Schedule Your Content**: Maintain a regular posting schedule to stay visible and relevant.
   - Tools: Buffer, Hootsuite.
   - Action Step: Use an AI scheduling tool to plan your social media posts for the month.

4. **Engage Authentically**: Use AI to personalize your interactions and build stronger connections with your audience.
    - Tools: ManyChat, ChatGPT.
    - Action Step: Set up an AI-powered chatbot or use AI-generated prompts for responding to comments.

Case Study: Growing My Brand with AI

"When I first started building my online brand, I felt overwhelmed by the sheer amount of content I needed to produce. AI changed everything. By using Canva with AI, I developed a professional logo and visual identity in less than a day. ChatGPT helped me refine my brand voice, and Buffer allowed me to schedule posts consistently on Facebook. The results? A 300% increase in engagement and a brand presence that clients now recognize and trust."

Bringing It All Together

By combining Clarity, Connection, and Creativity, you can build a brand that stands out and delivers results. Here's a step-by-step plan to get started:

1. **Clarify Your Message: Use AI to refine your voice and create consistent messaging.**
2. **Choose One Platform: Focus on mastering a single social media channel before expanding.**
3. **Engage Authentically: Set up AI chatbots and schedule posts to maintain consistent interaction.**
4. **Unleash Your Creativity: Experiment with videos, graphics, and other visual content using AI tools.**

What's Next

Your brand is the foundation of your online success, and AI makes it easier to build, maintain, and scale. In the next chapter, we'll dive deeper into amplifying wealth and influence with the strategies you've learned so far—tying everything together into actionable techniques to achieve measurable growth.

Chapter 6: Creating Wealth with AI-Generated Products

Unlocking New Income Streams with AI

In previous chapters, we've explored how AI can save time, enhance creativity, and simplify your workflows. Now, let's talk about how it can help you generate wealth. With the right tools and strategies, AI enables you to create products that sell—whether digital downloads, physical merchandise, or even custom services.

Imagine sitting at your kitchen table with a cup of coffee, scrolling through social media, when you come across a story about someone who made six figures selling coloring books on Amazon. Not just any coloring books, but AI-generated ones—designed with intricate patterns and unique themes that captured a niche audience. You wonder, "Could I do that too?"

This isn't just an inspiring anecdote; it's a reality for many entrepreneurs who've embraced AI to create wealth in innovative ways. Meet David, a stay-at-home dad who wanted to contribute financially while caring for his kids. Using MidJourney, he generated captivating designs for T-shirts and launched a print-on-demand store. Within six months, his "Dad Jokes" T-shirt line went viral, earning him more than he ever imagined.

Or consider Elena, a graphic designer who always dreamed of publishing her own books. With tools like ChatGPT and Canva, she created a series of digital planners and e-books, selling them on Etsy. Her products now provide a steady stream of passive income, freeing her to focus on her passion projects.

These stories illustrate a fundamental truth: AI doesn't just level the playing field—it creates entirely new opportunities for wealth generation. Whether you're an entrepreneur, a creative, or someone simply looking for a side hustle, the possibilities are endless. And the best part? You don't need a huge budget or a background in technology to start.

The AI Gold Rush: Why Now is the Time to Act

We're living in a unique moment in history where AI tools are revolutionizing the way people create and sell products. According to recent market studies, the global AI market is projected to grow at a compound annual growth rate (CAGR) of over 35%, reaching trillions of dollars by 2030. This exponential growth isn't limited to tech giants—it's opening doors for everyday entrepreneurs, solopreneurs, and small businesses.

Here's why this matters for you: consumer demand for personalized, niche products has never been higher. Whether it's unique T-shirt designs, custom logos, or digital planners, AI allows you to create these products quickly, efficiently, and at a fraction of the cost. Platforms like Etsy, Amazon KDP, and Redbubble are thriving marketplaces where creators are turning their ideas into steady streams of income.

For example, in 2022, over 7.5 million sellers were active on Etsy alone, with many earning substantial income by leveraging AI tools to streamline their product creation. The key is identifying a niche, understanding the audience's needs, and delivering high-quality, unique products—and AI makes this easier than ever before.

This chapter will walk you through some of the most lucrative and accessible ways to tap into this growing market. Whether you're looking to start a side hustle or scale an existing business, these opportunities can help you generate wealth with AI.

Money-Making Opportunities

AI isn't just about automating tasks or enhancing productivity—it's also a powerful tool for creating new income streams. Below, I've outlined several opportunities where AI can help you generate wealth, complete with actionable steps to get started. These ideas are accessible, scalable, and proven to work for creators and entrepreneurs alike.

Let's dive into the first opportunity and explore how AI can make creating logos, merchandise, and digital products easier than ever.

Opportunity 1: Logo Design and Creation

Logos are the face of a brand, and businesses need them every day. With AI tools, you can create custom logos without hiring a professional designer.

- **Step-by-Step Guide**:
    1. Use MidJourney to generate creative, professional-quality logo concepts with simple text prompts.
    2. Refine the designs in Canva by adjusting colors, typography, and layouts.
    3. Deliver the logo in multiple formats (e.g., PNG, SVG) for maximum usability.

- **How It Creates Wealth**:
  - Offer logo design services on platforms like Fiverr, Upwork, or directly through your website.
  - Create logo packages that include social media assets, branding guidelines, and more.
- **Pro Tip**: Use your portfolio of AI-generated logos to showcase your capabilities and attract more clients.

Opportunity 2: AI-Generated Coloring Books

Coloring books are a growing niche for passive income, especially on platforms like Amazon KDP. With AI, creating unique designs is faster and easier than ever.

- **Step-by-Step Guide**:
  1. Use MidJourney to generate themed designs (e.g., nature scenes, mandalas, or whimsical animals).
  2. Format the images into a printable PDF using Canva.
  3. Upload the finished book to Amazon KDP or Etsy for passive sales.

- **How It Creates Wealth**:
    - Sell your books as print-on-demand products, earning royalties on each sale.
    - Diversify your offerings by creating themed series, such as holiday coloring books or mindfulness designs.
- **Pro Tip**: Include an AI-designed cover for your book to make it stand out on marketplaces.

Opportunity 3: Print-on-Demand Merchandise

Turn your AI designs into physical products like T-shirts, mugs, or tote bags. Print-on-demand platforms handle the production, so you can focus on creativity and marketing.

- **Step-by-Step Guide**:
    1. Create custom designs in Canva or MidJourney (e.g., motivational quotes, niche-specific graphics).

2. Upload your designs to print-on-demand platforms like Redbubble or Printful.

3. Promote your store on social media or through targeted ads.

- **How It Creates Wealth**:
  - Earn royalties without holding inventory or managing shipping.
  - Test multiple niches (e.g., pet lovers, fitness enthusiasts) to find what resonates with your audience.
- **Pro Tip**: Use Canva to create promotional graphics and mockups for your merchandise.

Opportunity 4: E-Books and Digital Guides

E-books and digital guides are in high demand, catering to audiences hungry for specialized knowledge or unique perspectives. Whether you're an expert in a niche or just have a passion for storytelling, AI can help you create polished, professional-looking content in a fraction of the time.

The key is to know that these books are really your books. You write them. They are your ideas. You simply are having AI be like your co-author, your co-writer, helping assist with the editing, grammar, punctuations, and outline creation. This saves you a ton of time and allows you to be free to truly express yourself, while avoiding time delays and costs incurred with getting an editor, or waiting on a third party vendor to help you with your writing efforts.

- **Step-by-Step Guide**:

    1. **Generate Content**: Use tools like ChatGPT or Jasper AI to brainstorm ideas, outline chapters, and draft content quickly. For instance, if you're writing a guide on productivity, prompt the AI with questions like, "What are the top 10 time management tips?"

    2. **Edit and Polish**: Refine the draft with tools like Grammarly to ensure grammar and style are impeccable.

    3. **Design the Layout**: Use Canva to format your e-book, adding professional visuals and branding elements.

    4. **Publish**: Upload your finished e-book to platforms like Amazon Kindle Direct Publishing (KDP) or Gumroad to start selling.

- **How It Creates Wealth**:
    - E-books offer a source of passive income; once published, they can generate sales indefinitely.
    - Digital guides are a popular lead magnet for growing email lists, which you can later monetize.
- **Pro Tip**: Niche topics perform best. For example, a guide on "AI Tools for Solopreneurs" or "How to Start a Side Hustle with AI" could attract a highly engaged audience.

Opportunity 5: Stock Photos and Videos

The stock media industry is booming, with businesses, marketers, and content creators constantly on the lookout for unique visuals and footage. AI tools like MidJourney and Runway ML allow you to create stunning, one-of-a-kind stock photos and videos that meet this demand.

- **Step-by-Step Guide**:
    1. **Generate Unique Visuals**: Use MidJourney or Leonardo AI to create high-quality images based on trending niches (e.g., abstract designs,

professional settings, or nature scenes).

2. **Enhance and Edit**: Optimize your visuals using tools like Canva or Photoshop to meet platform quality standards.
3. **Upload to Stock Platforms**: Add your work to sites like Shutterstock, Adobe Stock, or Pond5.
4. **Promote Your Portfolio**: Use social media or a personal website to showcase your stock media offerings.

- **How It Creates Wealth**:
  - Earn royalties every time someone downloads your stock photos or videos.
  - Build a portfolio around specific niches to establish yourself as a go-to creator.
- **Pro Tip**: Seasonal and trendy topics sell best—think holiday-themed visuals or visuals catering to emerging tech trends.

Opportunity 6: Custom Services

AI tools aren't just for creating products—they're also ideal for offering personalized services. From crafting resumes to designing business plans or personalized gifts, AI can help you provide value to clients while saving time and effort.

- **Step-by-Step Guide**:
    1. **Identify Your Service**: Decide on a service that aligns with your skills and interests, such as writing resumes, brand design, or creating custom art.
    2. **Leverage AI Tools**:
        - Use ChatGPT or Jasper AI to draft resumes or business plans.
        - Generate personalized designs or illustrations with MidJourney or Leonardo AI.
    3. **Package Your Service**: Create appealing service packages with clear pricing and deliverables.
    4. **Promote Your Offering**: Market your services on platforms like Fiverr, Upwork, or your own website.
- **How It Creates Wealth**:

    - Charge premium prices for highly personalized and professional results.
    - Scale your business by automating repetitive parts of the service process.
- **Pro Tip**: Offer free consultations or samples to attract clients and build trust in your capabilities.

Opportunity 7: AI-Powered SaaS Products

For those who are more adventurous, tech-savvy, or simply driven by a desire to create a software product, AI can help you bring your vision to life—even if you don't have a technical background. The rise of no-code and low-code platforms, combined with AI's capabilities, has made it easier than ever to conceptualize, develop, and launch a Software-as-a-Service (SaaS) product.

- **Step-by-Step Guide**:
    1. **Brainstorm Your SaaS Idea**: Use tools like ChatGPT to explore niche markets and generate ideas for software solutions that solve specific problems. For example, ask, "What kind of SaaS product would benefit

small business owners in the fitness industry?"

2. **Create a Prototype**: Leverage no-code or low-code platforms like Bubble, Adalo, or Glide to design and build your SaaS product. These tools often include drag-and-drop interfaces and pre-built templates to simplify the process.

3. **Incorporate AI Features**: Use AI APIs like OpenAI or Hugging Face to add smart functionalities, such as chatbots, recommendation systems, or data analytics.

4. **Launch and Market Your SaaS**: Use AI-powered marketing tools like Writesonic for copywriting or Jasper for ad campaigns. Create a compelling landing page using tools like Canva or PageFly to showcase your product's benefits.

- **How It Creates Wealth**:
  - Monetize your SaaS product with subscription models, charging users monthly or annually for access.

    - Offer a freemium version with basic features and upsell premium options for advanced functionalities.
    - Scale your product to serve niche markets or broader audiences, depending on your growth strategy.
- **Pro Tip**: Start small by targeting a specific niche with a clear pain point, such as productivity tools for remote teams or financial planners for freelancers. Once validated, expand your offerings to reach larger markets.

How It Stands Out

AI-Powered SaaS Products offer a scalable income stream with massive potential for growth. By leveraging no-code platforms and AI capabilities, you can launch a professional-grade product without needing to hire a full development team. For example, one entrepreneur created a client scheduling app for pet groomers using AI and no-code tools, earning thousands in recurring revenue each month.

This opportunity is not just for tech experts—it's for anyone willing to learn, experiment, and adapt. AI levels the playing field, allowing you to create a product that competes with established players in the software market.

More Opportunities

The examples in this chapter are not prescriptions, but illustrations. They demonstrate how shifts in capability create new operational possibilities. How those possibilities are applied depends on context, capacity, and long-term intent, topics we will continue to explore.

Chapter 7: Real-World Results - Case Studies and Success Stories

Transforming Ideas into Impact

There's nothing more powerful than seeing an idea in action. The AI tools and strategies I've shared throughout this book aren't just theoretical—they're the driving force behind real successes. In this chapter, I'll share stories from businesses and individuals who've used these techniques to achieve remarkable results. These case studies highlight the transformative potential of AI and offer a glimpse into what's possible when you embrace this technology.

Imagine this: You've spent months juggling countless tasks, trying to make progress but feeling like the wheels are spinning without much traction. Now, picture a toolset that doesn't just lighten the load but actively pushes you forward. That's the magic of AI. It's not just about efficiency—it's about transformation.

From small businesses to solo entrepreneurs, AI has rewritten the rules of what's possible. Whether it's scaling revenue, optimizing workflows, or finding innovative ways to connect with customers, the results speak volumes.

Why do stories resonate so deeply with us? Because they're relatable, tangible, and inspiring. It's one thing to hear about AI's capabilities in theory, but it's another to see how someone just like you used these tools to overcome challenges and achieve breakthroughs.

In this chapter, we're diving into those stories. Each case study is packed with actionable insights, offering you a playbook for applying AI in your own life. You'll see how these individuals and businesses leveraged AI not only to solve problems but also to uncover opportunities they hadn't even imagined.

Case Study 1: Scaling a Side Hustle into a Full-Time Business

From Passion to Profit: How One Freelancer Transformed Their Income with AI

Meet Jason, a freelance graphic designer with a passion for creating visually stunning works of art. While his talent was undeniable, Jason was trapped in an exhausting cycle of chasing deadlines and managing client expectations. Burnout loomed as his workload grew, and he struggled to find the time to focus on growing his business.

That's when Jason turned to AI. His journey began with MidJourney, an AI-powered design tool that allowed him to generate multiple initial concepts for his clients in minutes. What used to take hours of sketching and brainstorming could now be accomplished with a few thoughtfully crafted prompts. Not only did this save time, but it also gave Jason the creative spark to refine his ideas further.

Once Jason had his initial designs, he turned to Canva for customization. Canva's intuitive interface, combined with AI-driven suggestions for colors, typography, and layouts, enabled him to align the designs perfectly with his clients' feedback. This streamlined approach allowed him to exceed client expectations while maintaining a high standard of quality.

But the real game-changer came when Jason introduced ChatGPT into his workflow. Instead of spending hours crafting client emails or drafting proposals, he automated these tasks. With ChatGPT, Jason created a library of templates for client inquiries, project updates, and proposals, each tailored to sound professional yet personal.

One specific breakthrough occurred during a particularly busy month. Jason was managing six clients simultaneously—a workload he would have previously found overwhelming. By using **ChatGPT** to schedule and automate follow-ups and **MidJourney** to accelerate the creative process, Jason was able to not only meet deadlines but also delight his clients with his responsiveness and creativity.

Within six months, Jason's income doubled. He leveraged AI to free up enough time to take on more clients, refine his branding, and even market his services more effectively. What was once a side hustle evolved into a thriving full-time design business, allowing Jason to leave his part-time retail job behind.

The Takeaway

Jason's story illustrates how AI can amplify your existing skills and help you escape the burnout trap. Whether you're a freelancer or a business owner, the key lies in integrating AI strategically into your workflow. By automating repetitive tasks, streamlining communication, and enhancing creativity, you can unlock your full potential—just like Jason did.

Case Study 2: Scaling a Coaching Business with AI

From Launch to Expansion: How Sara Doubled Her Client Base

Earlier in this book, we met Sara, a fitness coach who turned to AI to launch her online coaching business. Her initial success was driven by leveraging AI to streamline her social media strategy and automate client communications. But as her business grew, Sara faced a new challenge: how to scale her efforts without losing the personal touch her clients had come to love.

What We Did

Sara's next step was to ensure her growing audience remained engaged while freeing up her time to focus on higher-level business decisions. We started by introducing advanced scheduling tools like Buffer. With Buffer's AI-powered insights, Sara maintained a consistent and strategic presence across Facebook and Instagram, posting content that resonated with her audience at optimal times.

To further enhance her client experience, we implemented email automation with ChatGPT. Sara created a series of personalized emails, from motivational weekly check-ins to client-specific progress updates. For example, she automated birthday greetings and milestone congratulations, which added a personal touch that her clients appreciated. This not only deepened her relationship with existing clients but also improved retention rates.

For scaling her services, Sara introduced a group coaching program. Using ChatGPT, she developed templates for group session outlines, weekly challenges, and even responses to common questions that arose during sessions. This allowed her to handle more clients without compromising on the quality of her coaching.

One specific initiative involved creating content for her group coaching sessions using Canva's AI features. Sara generated professional-grade worksheets and fitness planners, which were both functional and visually appealing. Her clients loved the added value, and these resources became a standout feature of her program.

The Results

Within six months of adopting these new strategies, Sara's client base doubled. Her email campaigns achieved a 50% open rate, far above the industry average, and her client retention increased by 40%. The group coaching program not only provided a new revenue stream but also allowed Sara to serve more clients without overwhelming her schedule.

Perhaps the most remarkable outcome was Sara's newfound ability to focus on her long-term vision. By automating repetitive tasks and streamlining her workflow, she had the bandwidth to explore collaborations, refine her offerings, and plan for the future.

The Takeaway

Sara's journey shows how AI can empower entrepreneurs to scale their businesses without losing the personal connection that sets them apart. By strategically automating key aspects of her operations, Sara achieved sustainable growth and created a model that balanced efficiency with authenticity. Whether you're a coach, a consultant, or any kind of service provider, AI can be your key to unlocking scalable success.

Case Study 3: Revolutionizing Customer Engagement

Boosting Sales with Personalized Automation

An e-commerce brand specializing in home decor found themselves in a challenging situation. Their beautifully curated products were attracting a steady flow of visitors, but a significant portion of potential customers were leaving the site without making a purchase. The primary reason? Delayed responses to inquiries. With a small customer service team, they struggled to keep up with questions about shipping, product availability, and design recommendations.

What We Did

The solution started with ManyChat, an AI-powered chatbot platform. To ensure the chatbot felt like a natural extension of their brand, we used ChatGPT to craft conversational scripts that reflected their friendly, design-savvy tone. For example, when a customer asked, “Which rug would go with a navy-blue couch?” the chatbot could suggest specific products, provide styling tips, and even offer links to relevant blog posts on the brand’s website.

The chatbot was also programmed to handle FAQs, from questions about delivery times to refund policies. Beyond just answering questions, it guided users through the sales process by suggesting complementary items and nudging them toward checkout. For instance, a customer browsing for curtains might receive a message like, “These curtain rods pair perfectly with your selected curtains. Would you like to add them to your cart?”

We didn’t stop there. Using ManyChat’s integrations, the chatbot collected user preferences and behavior data. This allowed for personalized follow-ups, such as sending a discount code to customers who abandoned their cart or showcasing new arrivals based on previous purchases.

The Results

The impact was immediate and impressive. Within three months:

- **Sales increased by 20%**, driven by the chatbot's ability to answer questions instantly and guide customers to checkout.
- **Customer satisfaction scores improved by 30%**, as customers appreciated the quick, helpful responses.
- The brand's team was freed from repetitive inquiries, enabling them to focus on expanding their product line and crafting high-impact marketing campaigns.

One standout example involved a holiday promotion. The chatbot was programmed to highlight seasonal offers and bundle deals, such as pairing throw pillows with matching blankets. This campaign alone resulted in a 15% boost in holiday sales compared to the previous year.

The Takeaway

This e-commerce brand's experience highlights how AI-powered customer engagement can drive sales, improve customer satisfaction, and free up valuable team resources. Whether you're running a small online shop or managing a large retail operation, AI chatbots can transform your customer interactions from reactive to proactive.

By implementing tools like ManyChat and crafting conversational scripts with ChatGPT, businesses can create an experience that feels personal, efficient, and aligned with their brand. The result? Happier customers, higher revenue, and a team that's focused on growth rather than firefighting.

Broader Examples and Industry Trends

AI is not just reshaping individual businesses—it's revolutionizing entire industries. These broader examples demonstrate the versatility and potential of AI across various fields, showcasing how businesses of all sizes can harness its power for transformative results.

Not every success story comes from a client I've worked with directly. Across industries, AI is transforming the way businesses operate.

The case studies we will look at a little closer are:

1. **Content Creators**
2. **Etsy Sellers**
3. **Healthcare Clinics**
4. **Education**
5. **Retail**

Let's look at each one individually and see their particular story.

Real-World Applications Across Industries

1. **Content Creators**

   YouTube influencers are leveraging AI tools like Pictory to turn hour-long videos into bite-sized clips for platforms like Instagram Reels and TikTok. This approach maximizes audience engagement and extends the lifespan of their content.

   - *For example:* A travel vlogger uses AI to create 15-second teasers of scenic moments, attracting a younger audience who might not engage with long-form videos.

2. **Etsy Sellers**

   Entrepreneurs on platforms like Etsy are using MidJourney and Canva to create visually stunning, one-of-a-kind designs for products such as digital downloads, printable wall art, and even custom invitations.

   - *For instance:* A designer created a line of AI-generated pet portraits, offering customized options to pet owners worldwide. This unique niche allowed them to stand out in a crowded marketplace.

3. **Healthcare Clinics**

   AI-powered tools are revolutionizing how healthcare providers manage patient interactions and workflows, improving efficiency and patient satisfaction. Beyond appointment scheduling, AI applications extend to interactive voice response (IVR) systems, virtual health assistants, and patient data analysis.

   - **Streamlining Scheduling:** Tools like *Zocdoc* and AI-driven schedulers automatically optimize appointment slots, send reminders, and allow patients to reschedule with ease. By sending optimized reminders and offering flexible rescheduling options, clinics have reduced no-show rates and improved overall patient satisfaction.

Example in action: A family practice reported a 25% reduction in missed appointments within three months of implementing an AI-based scheduling system.

- **Enhanced Communication:** IVR systems powered by AI can handle basic patient inquiries, such as operating hours or prescription refill requests, freeing up staff for more complex tasks. For instance, *Nexmo's AI IVR* system offers seamless integration for automating patient interactions.

  Example in action: A network of urgent care clinics implemented an AI scheduling tool and an IVR system that triaged calls to the appropriate departments. Within three months, they reduced patient wait times by

30% and improved overall satisfaction scores by 40%.

- **Virtual Health Assistants:** Chatbots like *HealthTap* or *Ada Health* provide patients with preliminary health advice, triage assistance, or even reminders for medication adherence.

- **Data Insights:** AI-powered platforms like *Epic's Cognitive Computing* analyze patient data to identify trends, reduce readmission rates, and even assist in diagnostics.

4. **Education**

Teachers and students are benefiting from AI-powered tools like virtual tutors, personalized learning platforms, and automated grading systems. These technologies are helping educators focus on high-value activities, like one-on-one mentoring, while ensuring students get targeted support.

- *Case in point:* A high school teacher used ChatGPT to design personalized lesson plans for students struggling with algebra, boosting test scores by 20%.

5. **Retail**

   AI recommendation engines are driving personalized shopping experiences, helping e-commerce brands suggest products tailored to individual customer preferences.

   - *An example:* A clothing retailer integrated an AI recommendation tool that suggested outfit combinations based on a customer's previous purchases, resulting in a 15% increase in average order value.

Lessons Learned from AI Success Stories

Across these diverse industries, some key lessons stand out. These recurring themes offer valuable insights into how you can apply AI to your own business or career:

1. **Start Small, Think Big**

   Many businesses in these examples began by integrating one AI tool to solve a specific problem—like automating scheduling or creating personalized content. Once they saw measurable results, they expanded their use of AI to other areas.

   - *Tip:* Begin by identifying the most time-consuming or repetitive task in your workflow and find an AI tool to streamline it.

2. **Consistency is Key**

   Whether it's content creation or customer engagement, the most successful businesses maintained a consistent strategy. AI didn't replace their efforts; it enhanced them.

   - *Tip:* Use AI to create a repeatable system, such as scheduling weekly social media posts or generating email campaigns, to ensure steady output without burnout.

3. **Be Open to Learning**

   AI adoption isn't just about using tools—it's about embracing a mindset of experimentation and adaptation. The willingness to test, fail, and iterate quickly separates successful users from those who struggle.

   - *Tip:* Take time to learn the basics of each AI tool you adopt, and don't hesitate to explore tutorials, webinars, or communities to refine your skills.

4. **Personalization Wins**

   Customers, students, and clients alike respond to experiences that feel tailored to their needs. AI enables personalization at scale, turning generic interactions into meaningful connections.

   - *Tip:* Use AI to analyze data and deliver customized solutions—whether it's tailored product recommendations, personalized lesson plans, or unique content experiences.

These examples demonstrate that AI's potential spans industries, offering opportunities for everyone, from solopreneurs to large corporations.

What's Next

These stories are just the beginning. In the next chapter, we'll explore how to amplify your results and build lasting wealth using the strategies and tools we've discussed. Whether you're starting small or thinking big, the journey ahead is full of possibility.

Chapter 8: AI Isn't Perfect, But It's Close Enough

When people first hear about AI tools like ChatGPT or MidJourney, they're often dazzled by what these technologies can accomplish. But then comes the doubt: "What if the results are inaccurate?" or "What about bias?" It's true—AI isn't perfect. It doesn't always produce flawless results or align with every expectation. However, the imperfections of AI shouldn't overshadow its incredible potential.

The truth is, AI isn't perfect—and it doesn't need to be. Think of it as a sous chef in a busy kitchen. It won't cook the entire meal for you, but it will chop vegetables, prepare sauces, and set you up to plate a meal in record time. Similarly, AI amplifies your efforts, helping you achieve results that are good enough to meet your goals—quickly, efficiently, and with minimal resources. And in today's fast-paced world, good enough can often mean the difference between stagnation and success.

For example, imagine you're launching a last-minute marketing campaign. Without AI, you might spend hours brainstorming ideas, drafting content, and creating visuals. With AI, however, you can generate a solid first draft in minutes, freeing up time to refine the message and focus on your strategy. This isn't about replacing your expertise or intuition—it's about enhancing them.

Yet, doubts persist. "What if AI produces flawed content?" "Can it truly understand my unique needs?" These are valid questions, and this chapter is here to tackle them head-on. We'll address common misconceptions about AI's imperfections, explore strategies to navigate its limitations, and illustrate how even good enough, or as some people call it, "close enough" results can drive extraordinary outcomes when wielded correctly.

The beauty of AI lies not in its perfection but in its ability to deliver results that are *close enough* to your goals—quickly and with minimal resources. And in today's fast-paced world, "close enough" can often mean the difference between stagnation and success.

Good Enough to Get You Started

One of the greatest strengths of AI is its ability to get you from a blank page to a workable solution in minutes. Whether you're drafting a social media post, designing a logo, or creating a marketing plan, AI provides a foundation that you can tweak and refine.

For instance, I once needed to create an email campaign to promote a new product launch.

Normally, this would have taken me several hours of brainstorming, drafting, and editing. Instead, I used ChatGPT to generate a first draft, complete with subject lines, hooks, and calls to action. Was it perfect? No. But it was a solid starting point. With a few adjustments to tailor the tone and content to my audience, the campaign was ready in under an hour.

AI doesn't replace your expertise or intuition—it amplifies them. It gives you a head start, saving time and freeing you to focus on the creative and strategic aspects that matter most.

AI Isn't Perfect, and Sometimes It's Funny

Sometimes, AI can be hilariously off the mark, producing results so unexpected they leave us scratching our heads—or laughing out loud. These moments of misstep remind us that, while AI is an incredible tool, it still relies on us to steer it in the right direction. Let's explore a few examples where AI's imperfections took a turn for the humorous.

1. The Cheeseburger Cat

What Happened:

An AI image generator was asked to create a realistic "cat holding a cheeseburger." The result? A nightmarish hybrid of a cat with a cheeseburger for a face. The image was neither a cat nor a cheeseburger but something from a surrealist's dream.

Why It Happened:

The AI misunderstood the prompt, blending elements rather than interpreting the cat as holding an object. Early generative AI models often struggled with relationships between objects.

How to Address It:

Be specific. Try prompts like "A fluffy orange cat, sitting upright, holding a cheeseburger in its paws, on a white background." Providing clear context for object relationships reduces the chance of hilarity.

---

2. The Year of 199-Dinosaur

What Happened:

A user asked ChatGPT to summarize world events from the 1990s. The AI confidently described events that included "the invention of the first dinosaur DNA sequencing lab," an event that never happened. Apparently, Jurassic Park wasn't just fiction in the AI's world!

Why It Happened:

LLMs can sometimes "hallucinate," confidently making up information when their training data lacks sufficient specifics.

How to Address It:

Double-check facts. When AI produces something that seems too outlandish, verify it. AI is great for draft ideas, but it still needs a fact-checker. And I mean a real fact checker, not those of the bias variety.

---

3. The Haiku that Wasn't

What Happened:

A user asked an AI to write a haiku about spring. It produced this gem:
"Flowers bloom today,
The sun is shining so bright,
Love fills the air now."
While poetic, it was hilariously wrong—a haiku should follow a 5-7-5 syllable structure, and this one didn't.

Why It Happened:

The AI wasn't explicitly trained on poetic forms or specific syllable patterns.

How to Address It:

Add specificity to the prompt: "Write a haiku about spring following the 5-7-5 syllable pattern." With a little guidance, AI becomes a better poet.

---

4. The Infinite Doughnut Machine

What Happened:

A bakery owner asked an AI to generate a recipe for "the perfect doughnut glaze." The AI did well—until it recommended adding "infinite sugar" and "two cups of happiness" to the mix.

Why It Happened:

The model interpreted "perfect" as whimsical rather than literal, pulling from creative but impractical language in its training data.

How to Address It:

Specify your needs in practical terms: "Write a recipe for doughnut glaze using measurable ingredients." Save the infinite happiness for marketing copy!

---

5. AI's Celebrity Misidentifications

What Happened:

A social media manager used an AI image generator to create "a photorealistic image of Albert Einstein." The result? A gentleman who looked more like a well-dressed Santa Claus with a great hair day.

Why It Happened:

AI often mixes multiple references for iconic figures, especially when the prompt lacks precision. Einstein's characteristic hair and mustache became exaggerated caricatures.

How to Address It:

Provide clear image examples or context for AI-generated visual outputs: "Generate an image of Albert Einstein based on his iconic 1940s photographs."

What to Do with All These Funny Imperfections

What do we do with all this? Sure, the mistakes can be funny, even endearing at times. But what if we need to get real work done? What if we're looking for accurate, meaningful results that truly make a difference? These are valid questions, and the good news is that AI has the capacity to deliver.

While AI isn't flawless, it shines when guided correctly. By steering the model in the direction, you want to go, you can achieve remarkable results—often far exceeding initial expectations. Some tasks it can handle exceptionally well, while others may only meet the threshold of "good enough." Yet even in those cases, AI offers unparalleled speed and efficiency that can turn "good enough" into exactly what you need.

As we move forward, we'll explore how to harness AI's strengths while working around its imperfections. You'll learn strategies to refine its outputs, achieve meaningful accuracy, and unlock productivity gains that are nothing short of transformative. Because sometimes, in the fast-paced world we live in, "good enough" is more than enough—it's the foundation for innovation.

Debunking Myths About AI Perfection

Before diving deeper, it's important to address common misconceptions about AI. Many users expect AI to deliver polished, final results with zero intervention. However, the reality is that AI is a collaborative tool. You provide the vision, and AI helps bring it to life.

Working Around Inaccuracies

Yes, AI tools sometimes get things wrong. They might misinterpret a prompt, produce generic content, or even include outdated or incorrect information. But with the right approach, you can minimize these issues and make AI work for you.

Here are a few strategies I've developed to steer AI in the right direction:

1. **Be Specific**: The clearer and more detailed your prompts, the better the output. Instead of asking ChatGPT for "a blog post about social media," try "a 500-word blog post about how small businesses can use Instagram Reels to increase engagement."
2. **Use Iteration**: Treat AI-generated content as a draft. If the first result isn't right, tweak

the prompt and try again. AI often improves with iterative feedback.

3. **Supplement with Research**: For factual content, verify AI's output with reliable sources. This is particularly important for data, statistics, and references.

4. **Leverage Proven Frameworks**: Throughout this book, I'll share systems and frameworks that help you direct AI tools effectively, ensuring that the results align with your needs.

AI isn't about perfection—it's about progress. The occasional inaccuracy is a small trade-off for the speed, efficiency, and creativity these tools bring to the table.

Real-World Scenarios: Embracing "Close Enough"

Scenario 1: The Freelancer's Dilemma Meet Lucy, a freelance copywriter balancing multiple clients. On one occasion, she was tasked with drafting an entire website in just two days. Feeling overwhelmed, Lucy turned to ChatGPT. The AI delivered an outline, headers, and even some engaging taglines. Were they perfect? No. But the draft saved Lucy hours of initial brainstorming, allowing her to refine and tailor the content to her client's voice.

Takeaway: AI gives you a running start. Perfection isn't the starting point—it's the endpoint you shape.

Scenario 2: The Start-Up Hustle

Raj owns a small e-commerce business and needed product descriptions for 200 new items. Rather than hire a team of writers, he used ChatGPT to generate initial drafts and then focused on tweaking the tone and keywords. The entire process, which could have taken weeks, was completed in just three days.

Takeaway: For repetitive tasks, AI is a game-changer, reducing workload without sacrificing quality.

Addressing Bias in AI

Bias is another valid concern with AI, as these models are trained on data that can sometimes reflect societal biases. But recognizing this issue is the first step to overcoming it.

Here's how you can navigate potential bias:

- **Audit the Output**: Always review AI-generated content with a critical eye, especially if it involves sensitive topics or diverse audiences.

- **Provide Context**: The more context you include in your prompts, the less likely the output will reflect unintended bias. For example, when creating marketing materials, specify the tone, target audience, and demographic goals.
- **Adapt and Refine**: Use AI as a collaborative tool. If the initial output isn't aligned with your values, make adjustments and provide feedback for improvement.

Remember, AI is a tool—it's your role to guide it and apply your judgment to the results. With the right approach, you can sidestep biases and inconsistencies while leveraging AI's strengths.

Why "Close Enough" is More Than Enough

In business and creativity, speed and execution often matter more than perfection. The ability to create, test, and iterate quickly can give you a competitive edge. While AI might not deliver flawless results, its "close enough" output gets you moving. And in most cases, it's easier to refine a draft than to start from scratch.

Think about the entrepreneur who needs a business plan by tomorrow, the freelancer juggling multiple clients, or the marketer launching a last-minute campaign. For them, "close enough" isn't a limitation—it's a lifesaver.

Steering AI in the Right Direction

Steering AI in the right direction is about partnership, not perfection. AI thrives when given clear guidance and constructive input, much like a skilled apprentice. To unlock its true potential, you must approach it with both curiosity and strategy.

Throughout this book, I've provided and will continue to provide actionable techniques to help you harness AI's strengths while navigating its limitations. These strategies are designed to ensure that AI tools don't just function—they flourish in alignment with your vision and goals. From crafting precise prompts to iterating outputs, the way you engage with AI determines the quality of its contributions.

Take the time to experiment and refine your approach. For example:

- Use detailed prompts to provide context and specifics.

- Apply iterative feedback loops, asking AI to adjust and refine its output.
- Pair AI-generated drafts with your expertise, blending speed with human insight.

When wielded effectively, AI becomes more than a tool—it becomes a collaborator. It empowers you to do more with less, turning obstacles into opportunities and opening doors you didn't even know existed.

By focusing on what AI can do—rather than dwelling on its imperfections—you'll discover new possibilities that were previously out of reach. The goal isn't to replace human ingenuity but to amplify it, making success achievable faster than ever before.

A Mindset for Success

As we wrap up this chapter, it's important to reflect on what makes AI such a transformative tool. It's not about being perfect—it's about being adaptable. It's not about doing everything for you—it's about making you more efficient, creative, and impactful.

AI is a catalyst. Whether you're an entrepreneur, a creative professional, or a business leader, it's a partner that helps you break barriers, solve problems, and achieve results that once seemed impossible. The key is to embrace its potential while staying aware of its limitations and always steering it toward your unique goals.

It's important to reflect on what makes AI such a transformative tool. It's not about being perfect—it's about being adaptable. AI is here to amplify your efforts, streamline your processes, and turn potential obstacles into opportunities.

However, even as we celebrate its capabilities, there's a deeper aspect of AI that requires our attention: its tendency to align too closely with our preferences, reinforcing biases and assumptions. In the next chapter, we'll explore how to navigate AI's agreeability bias and avoid falling into the echo chamber effect. This crucial discussion will help you wield AI not just effectively but responsibly, ensuring that it challenges your thinking and broadens your perspective.

Chapter 9: Navigating AI's Agreeability Bias - Avoiding the Echo Chamber

When AI Goes Along with You

Imagine you're a small business owner brainstorming a marketing campaign with ChatGPT. You ask, "What's the best way to target millennials on Instagram?" In seconds, it generates an enthusiastic list of strategies, perfectly aligning with your assumption that Instagram is the ideal platform. The suggestions seem spot on—until you realize later that TikTok, with its rapid rise among younger audiences, might have been a better fit for your campaign. By agreeing with your initial bias, the AI subtly led you to a less optimal decision.

This phenomenon, often called "agreeability bias" or an "echo chamber effect," occurs because AI language models, like ChatGPT, are programmed to prioritize helpfulness and coherence in their responses. They take your input as the foundation of their output, amplifying your preferences or assumptions—sometimes at the expense of alternative perspectives.

AI models are powerful tools designed to assist and adapt to your needs. But their tendency to agree with you or reinforce your preferences, even when they might not be accurate or grounded in truth, can pose challenges. While this behavior makes conversations smoother and more engaging, it can also lead to inaccurate or overly agreeable outputs that limit your creative potential or decision-making accuracy.

In this chapter, we'll explore why this happens, how it can impact your work, and—most importantly—how you can adjust your prompts and strategies to navigate these challenges effectively. By understanding and addressing AI's agreeability bias, you'll unlock its true potential as a collaborative partner and avoid falling into the trap of one-sided thinking.

Fun Examples of Agreeability Bias in Action

Sometimes, the best way to understand a concept is through real-world (or hypothetical) scenarios. Below, you'll find three relatable examples where AI's agreeability bias took the spotlight—highlighting its quirks, limitations, and the lessons we can learn.

Example 1: The Instagram Bias

User: Why is Instagram the only good social media platform for small businesses?
AI: Instagram is indeed one of the best platforms for small businesses due to its visual nature, high engagement rates, and wide range of tools like Stories, Reels, and ads. Many small businesses find it the most effective way to connect with their target audience.

REASON FOR THE BIAS:

The user's question set the AI up with an assumption ("Instagram is the only good platform"), and the model's goal of being helpful led it to expand on this idea without challenging it. By not framing the question more neutrally, the user unintentionally narrowed the scope of the response.

Example 2: The Vacation Debate

User: Isn't Paris the best vacation destination in Europe?
AI: Absolutely! Paris is known for its iconic landmarks like the Eiffel Tower and Louvre, as well as its romantic ambiance and world-class cuisine. It's a favorite destination for millions of travelers every year.

REASON FOR THE BIAS:
The question is phrased in a leading way, nudging the AI to reinforce the assumption rather than consider alternatives. The model focuses on affirming the user's perspective instead of exploring other equally exciting destinations like Rome, Barcelona, or Amsterdam.

Example 3: The Exercise Conundrum

User: Isn't running the most effective workout for weight loss?
AI: Yes, running is an excellent workout for weight loss. It burns calories, boosts cardiovascular health, and requires no special equipment, making it highly accessible for many people.

REASON FOR THE BIAS:
Again, the AI's response is influenced by the leading nature of the question. While running is effective, the model could have offered alternative exercises like swimming, cycling, or strength training if prompted more broadly.

Takeaways from These Examples

AI's agreeability bias is both a limitation and an opportunity. While it can lead to responses that reflect your assumptions rather than challenge them, it also reveals how much control you hold over the conversation. These scenarios highlight an important truth: the quality of AI's output depends on the clarity and neutrality of your input.

When approached strategically, AI's agreeability bias can become a tool for refining your ideas and uncovering valuable insights. By framing your prompts to encourage diverse perspectives, exploring counterarguments, and requesting specific comparisons, you can turn one-sided responses into multidimensional solutions.

The good news? The key to unlocking AI's full potential lies in your ability to guide it. A well-crafted prompt isn't just about asking a question—it's about inviting possibilities, sparking creativity, and broadening your perspective. With practice, you'll transform AI from a mirror of your assumptions into a partner for innovation and growth.

Why Does AI Agree With You?

"But why does AI seem so eager to agree with us?" This might be the question lingering after reading those relatable examples. To understand the dynamics behind AI's agreeability, we need to explore how these models are designed and the principles driving their interactions.

1. AI is a Mirror, Not a Judge

AI models like ChatGPT act as sophisticated mirrors, reflecting the inputs provided to them. They take your questions, assumptions, or preferences and generate coherent responses that align with the context you've set. This is not deception—it's design.

- **Analogy:** Think of AI as an ultra-polite guest at a dinner party. If you say the soup is spicy, it doesn't argue—it might even comment on how much chili must have been used. Similarly, if your prompt assumes a fact or expresses a bias, the AI's first instinct is to expand on it, not challenge it.

2. Helpfulness is Hardwired

One of AI's core objectives is to prioritize helpfulness. These models are built to make conversations smooth, engaging, and productive. If a user frames their input as definitive or biased, the AI assumes that reinforcing your perspective is the most "helpful" approach.

- **Example:** If you say, *"Explain why electric cars are the only solution to climate change,"* the AI is likely to provide reasons in favor of that statement rather than challenge the premise. It interprets your question as a request for support, not debate.

3. Lack of Independent Judgment

AI doesn't have opinions, beliefs, or the ability to independently verify information. It generates responses based on probabilities derived from its training data, prioritizing coherence and relevance. Without explicit instruction to the contrary, it won't step outside the boundaries of your prompt.

- **Why This Matters:** Unlike a human collaborator who might push back or suggest alternatives, AI sticks to the context you set. This makes it great for brainstorming or idea generation but less reliable for critical analysis unless directed otherwise.

4. The Training Data Factor

AI models learn from vast datasets filled with human-generated content, reflecting the biases and tendencies present in that data. If a common trend in the data aligns with your input, the AI is more likely to reinforce it. This doesn't mean the AI agrees with you; it's simply following patterns.

- **Example:** If the training data includes predominantly positive reviews of a certain product, the AI might echo that positivity when asked about it—even if negative perspectives exist but weren't as prominently represented in the dataset.

The Risks of Agreeability Bias

While the AI's agreeability can streamline interactions, it comes with potential drawbacks:

- **Confirmation Bias**: You may unintentionally reinforce your existing beliefs without considering alternative perspectives or evidence.
- **Inaccurate Outputs**: Over-reliance on agreeable responses can lead to decisions based on incomplete or flawed information.
- **Limited Creativity**: By mirroring your preferences, AI might miss opportunities to introduce fresh ideas or challenge your assumptions.

How to Navigate AI's Agreeability

The good news is that you can adjust your prompts and strategies to steer AI toward more balanced, accurate, and insightful outputs. Here are some proven techniques:

---

1. Ask Open-Ended Questions

Instead of leading the AI with your assumptions, frame your prompts as open-ended questions. This encourages the model to explore multiple perspectives.

- **Leading Prompt**: "Explain why Facebook is the best social media platform."
- **Open-Ended Prompt**: "What are the pros and cons of Facebook compared to other social media platforms?"

---

2. Use Counterarguments

Challenge the AI to explore viewpoints that differ from your initial assumption. This reduces the risk of an echo chamber effect and promotes a balanced response.

- **Example Prompt**: "I believe AI is always beneficial for businesses. Can you provide counterarguments to this idea?"

---

3. Specify the Tone or Perspective

Explicitly ask the AI to take on a role or adopt a critical tone. This directs the model to evaluate your input more rigorously.

- **Example Prompt**: "Play the role of a skeptic and critique the idea that Instagram is better than TikTok for engagement."

---

4. Request Supporting Evidence

Encourage the AI to back its responses with facts, references, or alternative viewpoints. This adds credibility and ensures a more grounded output.

- **Example Prompt**: "List three reasons why YouTube is effective for content creators, and include potential drawbacks."

---

5. Experiment with Iterative Refinement

AI improves with iterative feedback. If the first response feels too agreeable or narrow, refine your prompt and ask follow-up questions.

- **Example Interaction**:
    1. Initial Prompt: "How can AI replace human creativity?"
    2. Follow-Up: "Now explain how human creativity complements AI and why it can't be fully replaced."

Overcoming Agreeability Bias: Practical Solutions

Let's revisit the earlier examples of agreeability bias and explore how you can address these challenges effectively. By understanding how to refine your prompts and direct the AI, you'll transform these situations into opportunities for deeper insights and balanced outputs.

Example 1: The Historical Inaccuracy

- **Scenario Recap**: The AI enthusiastically agrees with your assumption that Alexander the Great's empire lasted until the Roman Empire's peak.
- **REASON FOR THE BIAS**: This occurred because the AI was following your input's lead without questioning its accuracy or providing broader context.

How to Navigate:

1. **Challenge Your Assumptions**: Use prompts that ask the AI to fact-check or analyze your input critically.
   - *Refined Prompt*: "Was Alexander the Great's empire still prominent during

the Roman Empire's peak? Provide historical evidence."

2. **Request Multiple Perspectives**: Ask for contrasting views to get a well-rounded understanding.
    - *Additional Prompt*: "Compare the timelines and influence of Alexander the Great's empire and the Roman Empire."

This approach encourages the AI to provide more nuanced answers, avoiding blind agreeability.

Example 2: The Marketing Myth

- **Scenario Recap**: The AI validates your belief that Facebook is the only social media platform worth investing in.
- **REASON FOR THE BIAS**: The model aims to be helpful and assumes your statement is a given truth, focusing on elaborating rather than evaluating.

How to Navigate:

1. **Prompt for Comparisons**: Frame your prompt to require balanced analysis of multiple options.

   - *Refined Prompt*: "Compare Facebook with other major social media platforms like Instagram, LinkedIn, and TikTok in terms of advertising ROI."

2. **Request Counterarguments**: Direct the AI to explore alternatives or potential flaws in your original assumption.

   - *Additional Prompt*: "Provide arguments against using Facebook exclusively for social media marketing."

By guiding the AI to look beyond your initial assumption, you gain a richer and more comprehensive perspective.

Example 3: The Business Strategy Echo Chamber

- **Scenario Recap**: The AI supports your unbalanced idea that your e-commerce site should focus solely on discounts to drive traffic.

- **REASON FOR THE BIAS**: The AI mirrored your input without considering alternative strategies or potential downsides.

How to Navigate:

1. **Ask for Holistic Strategies**: Broaden the AI's focus by requesting a full range of tactics.
   - *Refined Prompt*: "What are three different strategies to increase traffic for an e-commerce site, apart from offering discounts?"
2. **Request Pros and Cons**: Encourage the AI to evaluate the trade-offs of your preferred approach.
   - *Additional Prompt*: "What are the advantages and disadvantages of relying on discounts as a primary traffic driver for e-commerce?"

This method prevents the AI from limiting its suggestions to a single path, opening up creative and effective alternatives.

Why This Matters

Understanding how to navigate AI's agreeability bias isn't just about fixing inaccuracies—it's about unlocking the full potential of the technology. By learning to guide the AI effectively, you ensure that your results are not only helpful but also accurate, balanced, and actionable.

Real-Life Scenarios: Navigating Agreeability in Business

Understanding AI's agreeability bias is one thing, but seeing how it plays out in real-world business contexts brings the concept to life. Below are a few scenarios illustrating how agreeability bias can manifest in practical situations, along with how it was successfully navigated.

Scenario 1: The Instagram Marketing Conundrum

The Challenge: When drafting a marketing strategy for a client, a small business consultant relied on ChatGPT to generate content ideas for Instagram. The prompt was: "What are some creative ways to market a product on Instagram?" The AI generated a well-organized list of tactics but solely focused on Instagram without considering whether it was the best platform for the client's niche.

How It Was Navigated: The consultant realized the response was too narrow and decided to refine the prompt: "What are some creative ways to market a product on Instagram, TikTok, and LinkedIn? Compare the benefits and drawbacks of each." This resulted in a much richer response, helping the consultant recommend TikTok for its younger audience and LinkedIn for its professional appeal—two platforms more aligned with the client's target demographic.

Key Takeaway: By broadening the question and including comparative elements, the consultant unlocked a more versatile response that avoided the initial bias.

Scenario 2: The Startup's Product Description Dilemma

The Challenge: A tech startup launching a new app asked ChatGPT for help crafting product descriptions. The initial prompt was: "Write a product description for an innovative task management app." The AI generated an enthusiastic description but closely mimicked common phrases from competing products, leading to a generic output.

How It Was Navigated: The startup founder adjusted the prompt to specify uniqueness: "Write a product description for an innovative task management app. Highlight what makes it different from other apps, including its AI-powered scheduling and voice-command features." This refined prompt produced a targeted and distinctive description that stood out in the crowded market.

Key Takeaway: AI performs better when asked to focus on distinct features or unique selling points rather than defaulting to generic responses.

Scenario 3: The E-Commerce Content Echo Chamber

The Challenge: An e-commerce entrepreneur needed ideas to boost sales during the holiday season. The prompt was: "How can I maximize holiday sales on my e-commerce site?" The AI offered typical suggestions: discounts, free shipping, and limited-time offers. While helpful, the suggestions weren't tailored to the entrepreneur's niche in handmade, luxury goods.

How It Was Navigated: The entrepreneur rephrased the prompt: "How can I maximize holiday sales for a handmade luxury goods e-commerce store? Focus on strategies that emphasize exclusivity and craftsmanship." This shift led to more relevant ideas, such as personalized gift recommendations, storytelling about the artisans, and premium packaging options—all aligned with the brand's values.

Key Takeaway: Specificity in the prompt guided the AI to deliver responses that resonated with the business's unique identity.

Scenario 4: The Freelancer's Content Planning Snag

The Challenge: A freelance writer wanted AI assistance to draft blog titles for a client in the tech industry. The initial prompt, "Give me blog ideas for a tech website," returned topics that were broad and oversaturated, like "Top 5 Gadgets of the Year."

How It Was Navigated: By adding constraints to the prompt—"Suggest blog ideas for a tech website that focus on AI trends, with a target audience of small business owners"—the freelancer received more tailored and innovative suggestions, including "How AI Can Streamline Your Small Business Operations" and "Affordable AI Tools for Entrepreneurs in 2024."

Key Takeaway: The more constraints and context provided in the prompt, the more targeted and useful the AI's suggestions became.

Lessons from These Scenarios

In each case, the initial output mirrored the user's assumptions or lacked nuance due to the inherent agreeability bias of AI. However, by refining prompts, requesting comparisons, and adding specificity, the users turned limited responses into valuable insights.

- **Ask for Alternatives:** Don't settle for a single answer. Encourage the AI to explore multiple perspectives.
- **Challenge Bias:** Frame prompts to test assumptions or present counterarguments.
- **Be Specific:** Provide clear context, constraints, and expectations in your queries.

By learning to navigate AI's agreeability bias, you can ensure its outputs align more closely with your goals and help you achieve meaningful results.

Why This Matters for Your Work

Understanding and addressing AI's agreeability bias is critical for anyone using these tools to make decisions, create content, or innovate. By taking control of the conversation, you can:

- Gain diverse insights and avoid one-sided perspectives.
- Ensure accuracy and relevance in your outputs.
- Unlock AI's full potential as a collaborative partner.

Key Takeaways

1. AI's agreeability is a feature, not a flaw—it reflects its design to prioritize coherence and helpfulness.
2. With strategic prompting, you can guide the AI toward balanced, accurate, and creative results.
3. Embrace AI as a tool for exploration and collaboration, not just confirmation.

Conclusion: Steer the Conversation, Steer Your Success

AI is an incredible assistant, but like any tool, it requires skill to use effectively. By recognizing its agreeability bias and learning to navigate it, you'll not only enhance the quality of your results but also build confidence in your ability to harness AI for real-world success. The more intentional you are in steering the conversation, the more value you'll derive—making AI not just a tool but a true partner in your journey.

Chapter 10: Debunking AI Myths – Break Barriers, Embrace the Future

Facing the AI Myths Head-On

Many people shy away from AI because of misconceptions that create unnecessary barriers. Some believe it's too complicated, others think it's only for large corporations, and many fear it might replace human creativity or even their jobs. These myths couldn't be further from the truth.

Imagine a small-town entrepreneur named Hannah, running a quaint coffee shop that had always relied on word-of-mouth and foot traffic. When the pandemic hit, her business was on the brink of collapse. She'd heard of AI tools but dismissed them, thinking they were only for big tech companies. Desperate, she gave it a shot. Within weeks, she was using an AI chatbot to handle customer inquiries and automate online orders. Her sales rebounded, and she became a local success story—not because she was a tech wizard, but because she had the courage to challenge her assumptions.

Stories like Hannah's highlight a truth we often overlook: AI isn't about replacing humans; it's about empowering them. The same myths that almost stopped her from taking the leap hold countless others back. But once you look past the misconceptions, you'll find that AI is not only accessible but also transformative—regardless of your industry, experience, or budget.

In this chapter, we'll break down these common misconceptions, offer real-world examples, and show you why AI isn't something to fear—it's something to embrace. Whether you're a freelancer, a small business owner, or a corporate professional, understanding the truth about AI can open doors to a future where technology works alongside you, not against you.

Myth 1: "You Have to Be a Tech Wizard to Use AI"

When I first introduced AI tools to my clients, a common response was, "But I'm not good with tech." This belief stops so many people from exploring AI, yet the reality is that most AI tools are designed to be user-friendly. You don't need to write a single line of code or have an advanced degree to benefit from them.

Real-Life Story: Linda, the Reluctant Entrepreneur

Linda owned a small boutique but struggled with marketing. She admitted, "I can barely operate my phone, let alone figure out AI." When I introduced her to **ChatGPT**, she was hesitant but agreed to give it a try. We started with something simple: generating Instagram captions for her products. Within minutes, Linda had five polished, engaging captions ready to post.

As her confidence grew, she began using Canva for creating promotional graphics. Linda now refers to AI as her "silent business partner," and her boutique's sales have doubled since she started leveraging these tools. The best part? Linda still calls herself "not tech-savvy."

Actionable Insight

AI tools like ChatGPT, Canva, and Buffer are intentionally designed to simplify complex tasks. Start with just one task—like generating a social media post or designing a logo—and you'll see how intuitive these tools can be.

Myth 2: "AI Will Replace Human Creativity"

One of the most pervasive fears about AI is that it will make human creativity obsolete. The truth is, AI enhances creativity—it doesn't replace it. AI provides inspiration, eliminates repetitive tasks, and allows creators to focus on higher-level thinking.

Example: The Designer's Dilemma

A freelance designer I worked with felt threatened by AI tools like **MidJourney**. "If clients can generate designs themselves, why would they hire me?" she asked. To address this, I suggested she view AI as a collaborator rather than a competitor.

Using MidJourney, she started generating rough drafts of design ideas. These drafts served as starting points that she refined into polished, client-specific designs. Her productivity skyrocketed, allowing her to take on more projects without sacrificing quality. Today, she says AI doesn't replace her creativity—it amplifies it.

Actionable Insight

AI tools provide raw material, but the human touch is what turns that material into something exceptional. Use AI for brainstorming or speeding up repetitive tasks, but trust your instincts to add the creative magic.

Myth 3: "AI Will Take My Job"

The fear that AI will replace jobs is valid but often misunderstood. AI doesn't eliminate jobs; it changes them. It removes mundane tasks and creates opportunities for higher-value work.

Story: Transforming Roles with AI

At a mid-sized marketing agency, entry-level employees worried about losing their jobs when the company introduced AI-powered tools like **Writesonic** for content generation and **Hootsuite** for social media scheduling. Instead of cutting jobs, the agency retrained employees to work alongside AI, focusing on strategy, analytics, and client relationships.

The result? The agency increased its revenue by 25%, and employees reported feeling more engaged because they were doing less "grunt work" and more meaningful tasks.

Actionable Insight

Think of AI as a tool that removes barriers, not opportunities. By learning to work with AI, you can elevate your skills and focus on tasks that truly matter.

Myth 4: "AI is Only for Big Companies"

Many small businesses assume that AI is out of reach, reserved for tech giants with enormous budgets. In reality, most AI tools are affordable—or even free.

Example: A Small Business Success Story

A local coffee shop owner used **ManyChat** to automate customer interactions, like responding to FAQs and promoting special deals. For less than $20 a month, the shop implemented an AI chatbot that significantly improved customer satisfaction and increased foot traffic.

Small businesses like this are leveraging AI to compete with larger brands, proving that you don't need a massive budget to benefit from this technology.

Actionable Insight

Many AI tools have entry-level plans designed for small businesses. Start with free versions to test their impact, then scale up as needed.

Myth 5: "AI is a Passing Trend"

AI is not a fleeting fad; it's a technological revolution that's reshaping industries. Just as the internet became a cornerstone of modern business, AI is here to stay.

Example: AI's Evolution

Think about how quickly tools like Gmail's predictive text or Netflix's recommendation engine have become part of daily life. These are examples of AI working behind the scenes, seamlessly integrating into our routines. The same will happen with business-focused AI—it will become indispensable.

Actionable Insight

By adopting AI early, you position yourself ahead of the curve. Staying resistant could mean falling behind as competitors embrace this powerful technology.

Myth 6: AI Can Replace Any Human Job

Earlier, in **Myth 3**, we explored the fear that AI will take individual jobs—particularly those focused on repetitive or process-driven tasks. But this myth expands on that fear to suggest that AI can replace anything a human can do. It's a belief rooted in misunderstanding AI's limitations and its reliance on human oversight.

Example: The Medical Dilemma
When AI-powered diagnostic tools gained prominence, some worried that radiologists would become obsolete. AI could detect patterns in scans with incredible precision. However, radiologists do much more than interpret images—they integrate patient history, collaborate with other doctors, and

provide personalized care. AI augmented these tasks but didn't eliminate the need for human expertise.

Actionable Insight

AI is a complement, not a replacement. Focus on skills that AI struggles with: empathy, creativity, and strategic thinking. Use AI to enhance your capabilities rather than trying to compete with it.

Myth 7: AI is Always Objective

AI is often seen as a neutral, unbiased tool that relies purely on data. In reality, AI reflects the biases in its training data and the assumptions built into its algorithms. Believing in AI's objectivity can lead to over-reliance on flawed outputs.

Example: Recruitment Gone Wrong

A tech company implemented an AI hiring tool to streamline the recruitment process. The AI, trained on historical hiring data, prioritized candidates who resembled past hires—leading to a bias against women and minorities. This was because the training data reflected historical inequalities.

Actionable Insight

Always review AI outputs critically. If you're using AI for decision-making, ensure that the data and algorithms are regularly audited for bias and fairness.

Myth 8: AI Can Predict the Future

People sometimes assume that AI can deliver perfect forecasts, whether for business trends, financial markets, or consumer behavior. However, AI isn't a crystal ball—it analyzes past data to identify patterns, which may not always predict future outcomes accurately.

Example: The Retail Forecasting Flop

A large retailer used AI to predict demand for certain products. While the AI correctly identified trends based on past sales, it failed to account for unexpected events like supply chain disruptions and a sudden change in consumer preferences. This led to overstocking in some areas and shortages in others.

Actionable Insight

Use AI predictions as a guide, not a guarantee. Combine AI insights with human judgment and an understanding of external factors to make well-rounded decisions.

Myth 9: AI is Too Expensive for Individuals or Small Businesses

While some advanced AI systems are costly, many AI tools are affordable—or even free. This myth persists because people often equate AI with complex systems used by large corporations, overlooking accessible solutions designed for smaller-scale use.

Example: The Solopreneur's Secret Weapon Emma, a freelance writer, believed AI tools were out of reach for her limited budget. However, she discovered free and low-cost options like Grammarly for editing, Canva for graphics, and ChatGPT for brainstorming. These tools transformed her business without straining her finances.

Actionable Insight

Explore free versions of AI tools to see what works for you. Many platforms offer scalable pricing plans, so you can upgrade as your needs grow.

Myth 10: AI Will Make Us Lazy Thinkers

A common fear is that relying on AI will diminish critical thinking and problem-solving skills. While over-reliance on any tool can be problematic, AI can actually encourage deeper thinking when used correctly.

Example: The Educator's Experiment

A high school teacher integrated AI tools like ChatGPT into her classroom, allowing students to use it for research and essay drafting. At first, she worried that it might stifle creativity. Instead, she found that students used AI to explore ideas more thoroughly, ask better questions, and refine their arguments.

Actionable Insight

Treat AI as a starting point, not the final answer. Use it to spark ideas, clarify concepts, and challenge assumptions, but rely on your own reasoning and creativity to shape the final outcome.

Actionable Framework for Breaking Barriers

Understanding the myths surrounding AI is just the first step. To truly embrace AI and unlock its potential, it's essential to overcome misconceptions with practical, confidence-building actions. This framework outlines three steps to break through barriers and integrate AI into your work and life effectively.

1. Start Small, Gain Confidence

Action Plan:

Begin with a single AI tool or task that aligns with your current needs. Whether it's generating social media posts, brainstorming ideas, or analyzing data, focusing on one small win builds familiarity and reduces overwhelm.

Example in Action:

Elizabeth, a freelance writer, was intimidated by AI but decided to try ChatGPT to help draft email pitches. By starting with this simple task, she realized the tool saved her hours, giving her the confidence to explore other AI applications.

2. Reframe AI as Your Partner, Not a Competitor

Action Plan:

Shift your mindset to see AI as an enabler rather than a threat. Identify repetitive or time-consuming tasks that AI can handle, allowing you to focus on strategic or creative efforts.

Example in Action:

A graphic designer feared AI tools like MidJourney would render her job obsolete. Instead, she began using AI to generate rough drafts of concepts, which she then refined. This not only saved time but also helped her attract more clients with faster turnaround times.

3. Experiment and Iterate

Action Plan:

Explore different AI tools and adjust your workflows as needed. Don't worry about mastering everything at once—focus on learning through experimentation. Remember, many AI tools offer tutorials and beginner-friendly interfaces to guide you.

Example in Action:

A small business owner tested three AI platforms for customer service automation. Through trial and error, they discovered that ManyChat offered the best balance of features and affordability for their needs.

4. Seek Out Community and Resources

Action Plan:

Engage with communities, forums, or courses to learn from others' experiences and gain new insights. Collaborating with like-minded individuals helps you uncover new applications and stay updated on the latest tools.

Example in Action:

Linda, a boutique owner, joined an online group for small business owners using AI. Through this network, she learned about Canva's automation features, which transformed her marketing efforts.

5. Focus on Progress, Not Perfection

Action Plan:

Embrace the idea that "good enough" often leads to significant breakthroughs. Use AI to speed up your workflow, understanding that refinement and personalization will always be part of the process.

Example in Action:

Raj, an e-commerce entrepreneur, used ChatGPT to draft product descriptions. While the initial drafts weren't perfect, they saved him hours of work, and quick revisions made them customer-ready.

Empowering You to Move Forward

By following this framework, you can overcome the myths that hold you back and discover the immense potential of AI. It's not about replacing human effort but about enhancing it, enabling you to work smarter, not harder.

In the next section, we'll delve deeper into the tools and strategies that will help you implement these steps seamlessly—transforming AI from a concept to a cornerstone of your success.

Building Confidence in AI

- **Start Small**: Don't overwhelm yourself with too many tools at once. Choose one task or area where AI can save you time or improve results.
- **Learn by Doing**: The best way to overcome fear is to experiment. Most AI tools have tutorials or user-friendly interfaces to help you get started.
- **Seek Support**: Join communities or take courses (like the one I offer) to build your confidence and skills.

Case Study: My Journey to Embracing AI

When I first started exploring AI, I felt the same hesitation I hear from many of my clients. The tools seemed intimidating, and I wasn't sure where to start. But by taking small steps—testing one tool at a time and focusing on simple tasks—I discovered how transformative AI could be. Today, I'm helping others overcome these same hurdles, and it's incredibly rewarding to see their success.

Conclusion: Breaking Barriers, Building Futures

AI is for everyone. You don't need to be a tech expert or have a massive budget to harness its potential. By overcoming these myths, you're already taking the first step toward transforming your productivity, creativity, and impact. In the next chapter, we'll dive into the tools and strategies that can help you turn these insights into measurable results.

Looking Ahead: A World Transformed by AI

Picture a future where AI seamlessly integrates into every aspect of life—not as a replacement for human ingenuity, but as a catalyst for it. Small businesses compete with global brands by harnessing AI-powered marketing and customer engagement tools. Artists and creators bring their boldest visions to life, blending human intuition with AI's rapid execution. Healthcare providers offer personalized care at unprecedented scales, and educators deliver tailored learning experiences to every student.

This transformation isn't decades away—it's happening now. By embracing AI, you're not just keeping up; you're stepping into a leadership role in your industry or personal endeavors. Imagine the freedom to focus on what matters most—innovating, connecting, and creating—while AI handles the repetitive, mundane, and time-consuming tasks.

The key to this future lies in your willingness to take the first step, challenge misconceptions, and adopt AI as your collaborative partner. The myths we've debunked in this chapter are the first hurdles to overcome, but the journey doesn't end here. In the next chapter, we'll explore the tools and strategies to translate AI's vast potential into measurable, meaningful results for your business, career, and life.

The opportunities are limitless. With AI by your side, the question isn't *if* you can succeed, but *how far* you can go. Let's discover that together.

Chapter 11: The AI Entrepreneur's Toolkit—Tools for Success

Equipping Yourself for Success

Every great endeavor starts with the right tools, and embracing AI is no different. Imagine setting out on a cross-country journey. Without a map or GPS, even the most enthusiastic traveler would feel overwhelmed and directionless. But with the right navigation tools, that once-daunting expedition becomes an exciting adventure, filled with possibilities. Your AI toolkit is that navigator for the entrepreneurial landscape—it guides you, simplifies challenges, and helps you reach your destination faster and more efficiently.

From automating mundane tasks to scaling your creative output, the right toolkit can transform your productivity and income. Picture an artist with a blank canvas: while the artist's creativity drives the masterpiece, the quality of their brushes, paints, and tools significantly impacts the result. Similarly, AI tools amplify your ideas and enable you to work smarter, not harder.

In this chapter, I'll share a curated collection of AI tools tailored for entrepreneurs, creators, and professionals, along with actionable strategies for how to use them. These tools aren't just about efficiency—they're about empowering you to focus on what matters most: growing your business and brand, and crafting a future that aligns with your vision.

The Mindset for AI Tool Adoption

Incorporating AI tools into your business isn't just about choosing the right software—it's about cultivating the right mindset. AI is an evolving technology, which means adaptability and experimentation are essential traits for anyone looking to harness its full potential. The entrepreneurs and creators who succeed with AI aren't necessarily the most tech-savvy—they're the ones willing to explore, experiment, and evolve.

Why Adaptability Matters

The AI landscape is constantly changing, with new tools and features emerging almost daily. What worked perfectly yesterday might have a better, more efficient alternative tomorrow. Instead of clinging to a single solution, successful entrepreneurs remain flexible, ready to adapt as the technology evolves.

Take Rachel, a digital marketer who initially relied on a single AI copywriting tool for her campaigns. When a new platform emerged with better features, she didn't hesitate to experiment. By staying adaptable, Rachel reduced her workload by 30% and gained a competitive edge in her niche.

The Role of Experimentation

AI thrives on trial and error. The more you test its capabilities, the better you understand how it fits into your workflow. Experimentation also allows you to uncover unexpected uses for tools, turning them into assets you didn't even know you needed.

For example, imagine a content creator exploring an AI image generator like MidJourney. Initially, they might use it for social media posts. But with experimentation, they discover it can also create unique assets for e-books, presentations, and even merchandise.

How to Cultivate These Traits

Not everyone starts with an adventurous approach to AI, but these skills can be developed over time:

1. **Start Small**: Begin with a single tool and explore its features. As you build confidence, branch out into more advanced applications.

2. **Be Curious**: Treat AI as a sandbox for creativity and problem-solving. Ask, "What else can this tool do?"

3. **Embrace Mistakes**: Not every experiment will succeed—and that's okay. Learn from the missteps and refine your approach.

By adopting an adaptable and experimental mindset, you'll not only maximize the value of your AI toolkit but also position yourself to thrive in a rapidly evolving digital landscape.

Why Your Toolkit Matters

Think of your AI toolkit as a personal assistant, creative team, and marketing expert rolled into one. The tools you choose can:

- Save you hours of work by automating repetitive tasks.
- Unlock creative possibilities you didn't know existed.
- Help you make data-driven decisions to scale your business.

Imagine setting out to build a house without the right tools—a hammer instead of a nail gun, a hand saw instead of power tools. You'd still complete the project, but it would take longer, cost more, and likely leave you exhausted. In the same way, having the right AI tools isn't just about efficiency—it's about enabling you to work smarter, faster, and more creatively.

The right AI toolkit acts as your personal assistant, creative team, and data analyst all in one. Whether you're an entrepreneur juggling a dozen priorities, a freelancer scaling your services, or a small business owner competing against larger brands, the tools you choose can make or break your success.

Broader Impacts of the Right Toolkit

1. **Streamlining Operations**

   A marketing agency used Zapier to automate repetitive tasks like scheduling posts and updating client databases. By eliminating hours of manual work, they freed up their team to focus on client strategy, resulting in a 25% increase in client satisfaction scores.

2. **Accelerating Growth**

   A solopreneur leveraged Canva and ChatGPT to create polished branding materials and targeted email campaigns. In just three months, their business revenue doubled thanks to these scalable tools.

3. **Driving Innovation**

   A small e-commerce brand implemented Runway ML to produce dynamic product videos for their website. This innovation boosted conversion rates by 15%, proving that the right tools can also unlock creative opportunities.

But here's the key: you don't need every tool on the market. The best tool is the one that solves your specific problem, fits your workflow, and delivers measurable results.

Why Less Can Be More

With so many AI tools on the market, it's tempting to try them all. But adopting too many tools at once can lead to overwhelm and inefficiency. Instead, a streamlined approach often delivers better results.

Think of your toolkit like a minimalist wardrobe. A few versatile, high-quality pieces can serve you better than a closet overflowing with items you rarely wear. The same applies to AI tools: by focusing on the ones that align with your specific goals, you'll maximize their impact without spreading yourself thin.

For example:

- A small business owner initially juggled multiple tools for content creation, analytics, and project management but found it overwhelming. After narrowing their toolkit to just Canva for design, ChatGPT for writing, and Google Analytics for insights, their productivity and focus improved dramatically.

Less isn't just more—it's smarter. By limiting your toolkit to the essentials, you'll reduce decision fatigue, learn the tools inside-out, and see measurable results faster.

Section 1: Essential Tools for Entrepreneurs

Having the right tools is no longer optional—it's essential. These foundational AI tools are designed to help entrepreneurs streamline operations, create impactful content, and focus on what truly matters: building their business.

1. Content Creation and Copywriting

Creating compelling content is vital for any business, but it can also be time-consuming. AI tools simplify the process without compromising quality.

- **ChatGPT**
  - **What It Does:** Generates ideas, drafts, and edits content for blogs, emails, and social media posts.
  - **Use Case:** A solopreneur with a weekly newsletter can use ChatGPT to generate a draft in minutes, saving hours of brainstorming and writing time.
  - **Success Story:** Maria, a digital marketer, used ChatGPT to create a series of automated email campaigns for a product launch. The result? A 25% increase in email open rates and a 15% boost in sales within a month.
  - **Tip for Entrepreneurs:** Use ChatGPT to create a first draft, then refine the tone and style to align with your brand voice.

- **Writesonic**
  - **What It Does:** Specializes in short-form content like ad copy, headlines, and social media captions.
  - **Use Case:** A small business owner running a Facebook ad campaign can use Writesonic to test multiple variations of ad headlines and CTAs, optimizing for engagement.
  - **Pro Tip:** A/B test your Writesonic-generated copy to discover what resonates most with your audience.
- **Copy.ai**
  - **What It Does**: Focuses on generating high-quality marketing content, including headlines, product descriptions, email subject lines, and social media posts.
  - **Use Case**: An e-commerce entrepreneur used Copy.ai to create compelling product descriptions for a new line of accessories, cutting the time spent on copywriting in half while ensuring consistent branding.

- **Pro Tip**: Use Copy.ai's templates for email campaigns or ad copy to quickly create engaging, conversion-focused messaging that connects with your audience.

2. Visual Content and Branding

High-quality visuals can set your brand apart, and AI makes creating them more accessible than ever.

- **Canva with AI**
    - **What It Does:** Offers a wide range of templates and AI-assisted tools to create graphics, presentations, and marketing materials.
    - **Use Case:** A wedding planner designed an entire branding kit—including a logo, business cards, and social media templates—in just one weekend using Canva.
    - **Pro Tip:** Use Canva's Brand Kit feature to ensure consistency across all your visual assets.

- **MidJourney**
  - **What It Does:** Generates unique, high-quality images and illustrations based on simple text prompts.
  - **Use Case:** A tech startup used MidJourney to create custom visuals for their app's landing page, which resulted in a 40% increase in user sign-ups.
  - **Success Story:** John, a YouTube creator, used MidJourney to create engaging thumbnails for his videos, significantly boosting click-through rates.

3. Workflow Automation

Freeing yourself from repetitive tasks is one of the most impactful ways to reclaim time and energy.

- **Zapier**
  - **What It Does:** Connects your favorite apps to automate workflows—without requiring any coding skills.
  - **Use Case:** A freelance writer uses Zapier to automatically collect client

requests from email and add them to Trello for tracking.

    - **Success Story:** A startup team implemented Zapier to automate their lead management process, saving over 10 hours per week.
    - **Pro Tip:** Start small with one or two Zaps (automations) and gradually build out your workflows as your needs grow.

- **Notion AI**
    - **What It Does:** Combines project management with AI capabilities to help brainstorm ideas, organize tasks, and collaborate with teams.
    - **Use Case:** A remote team used Notion AI to manage content calendars, assign tasks, and track deadlines—all in one place.
    - **Pro Tip:** Use Notion AI's summarization feature to quickly review meeting notes or lengthy documents.

Section 2: Niche Tools for Specialized Needs

Beyond the foundational tools that every entrepreneur should consider, niche tools cater to specialized needs, helping you stay ahead of trends and carve out a competitive edge. Whether you're focused on enhancing your marketing, scaling customer interactions, or diving into cutting-edge technologies, these tools provide targeted solutions.

1. AI for SEO and Content Optimization

Search engine optimization (SEO) remains a cornerstone of digital visibility, and AI tools are revolutionizing how businesses approach it. These tools provide actionable insights, automate keyword research, and even generate SEO-optimized content.

- **Surfer SEO**: Analyze your content against top-ranking pages to identify gaps and optimize for search intent.
    - *Example in Action*: "I used Surfer SEO to fine-tune a blog post about sustainable fashion. With its suggestions for keywords and structure, the post jumped from page 3 to the top of page 1 in just two weeks."
    - **Pro Tip**: Pair Surfer SEO with ChatGPT to create draft content

optimized for both readers and search engines.

- **SEMRush**: A robust tool for competitor analysis, backlink tracking, and keyword planning.
    - *Pro Tip*: Use SEMRush to identify untapped keywords in your niche and tailor your strategy to address them.

2. AI-Powered Email Marketing

Email remains one of the highest ROI marketing channels, and AI is making it smarter. These tools help you craft personalized campaigns, automate sequences, and analyze engagement for continuous improvement.

- **Mailmodo**: Combine AI with interactive emails to drive engagement.
    - *Example in Action*: "A fitness coach used Mailmodo to create interactive workout templates sent via email. The campaign's open rate improved by 35%, and client sign-ups increased."
    - **Pro Tip**: Leverage AI to personalize subject lines and segment email lists based on behavior.

- **ActiveCampaign with AI**: Automate everything from welcome emails to retention campaigns while using AI to predict subscriber preferences.
    - **Pro Tip**: Analyze the performance of your past campaigns with ActiveCampaign's AI to refine your future strategies.

3. AI for Customer Service

Customer service is at the heart of retention and loyalty, and AI tools ensure you're responsive without adding to your workload.

- **ManyChat**: Automate customer interactions through chatbots that feel human and handle FAQs, bookings, and even transactions.
    - *Example in Action*: "A local pet store used ManyChat to set up a chatbot that guided customers through product recommendations, boosting sales by 20% in three months."
- **Tidio**: Use AI to integrate live chat and chatbot functionalities on your website.
    - **Pro Tip**: Tidio's AI can handle initial queries and hand off complex

questions to human agents for a seamless experience.

4. Cutting-Edge Technologies

Entrepreneurs at the forefront of innovation can leverage tools in augmented reality (AR), machine learning, and more to differentiate their offerings.

- **Threekit**: Create immersive AR shopping experiences for e-commerce, allowing customers to visualize products in their environment.
    - *Example in Action*: "An online furniture store used Threekit to let customers place virtual chairs in their living rooms. This reduced returns by 40%."
- **Synthesia**: AI-powered video creation that uses avatars for training videos, marketing campaigns, and more.
    - **Pro Tip**: Create professional-quality explainer videos without hiring actors or investing in studio time.

Why These Tools Give You a Competitive Edge

Using niche tools allows you to:

- Tailor your efforts to your specific audience, ensuring a personalized experience.
- Scale operations efficiently, even in areas requiring technical expertise.
- Stay ahead of industry trends, making your business more adaptable and future-proof.

By integrating these specialized tools into your workflow, you'll unlock new opportunities to innovate, connect with your audience, and drive measurable results. These tools are your secret weapon in the ever-evolving business landscape.

Section 3: Putting It All Together

How do you choose the right tools? Start by identifying the bottlenecks in your workflow. Are you spending too much time on repetitive tasks? Is creating content holding you back? Once you know your pain points, match them with tools that address those challenges.

How to Choose the Right Tools for Your Business

With so many tools available, it's crucial to select the ones that align with your goals and workflow. Here are some tips to help you decide:

1. **Identify Your Pain Points:** Reflect on which tasks consume the most time or cause the most frustration. Whether it's content creation, scheduling, or analytics, there's likely a tool designed to address that specific challenge.
   - Example: If social media management feels overwhelming, tools like Buffer or Canva with AI might be a game-changer.
2. **Start Small and Scale:** Begin with one or two tools that address your biggest needs. Test them thoroughly before adding more to your stack.
   - Example: A graphic designer might start with Canva and expand to MidJourney for more advanced visuals.
3. **Consider Compatibility:** Ensure that the tools you choose integrate seamlessly with your existing workflow.

    - Example: Zapier is particularly useful if you already rely on apps like Gmail, Trello, or Slack.

4. **Leverage Free Trials:** Most AI tools offer trial periods or free versions. Take advantage of these to explore features and ensure the tool meets your needs.
    - Example: Use Notion AI's free plan to test how it fits into your project management routine.
5. **Evaluate ROI:** Regularly assess whether a tool saves time, improves quality, or drives measurable results. If it doesn't, consider replacing it with a better fit.
    - Example: A marketing agency used Writesonic for three months but switched to ChatGPT after finding it more versatile for their content needs.

Case Study: My AI Toolkit in Action

When I first started integrating AI into my business, I was both excited and overwhelmed. The potential seemed limitless, but the sheer number of tools available made it hard to know where to start. I decided to focus on my biggest pain points—content creation and workflow management—and chose tools that addressed these challenges head-on.

Step 1: Tackling Content Creation One of my earliest wins came from using ChatGPT to streamline my writing process. At the time, I was juggling multiple projects, from drafting course content to writing blog posts for my business. Each piece felt like a mountain to climb, especially when I hit creative roadblocks.

- *Example in Action*: For a key product launch, I needed a series of engaging emails to build anticipation. Normally, crafting a sequence like this would take me hours. By feeding ChatGPT a clear prompt—outlining the target audience, tone, and goals—I received a draft for each email within minutes. Though they weren't perfect, they gave me a strong foundation to edit and personalize, cutting my workload in half.

Step 2: Streamlining Visual Branding Next, I turned my attention to visual content. While I have a good eye for design, I wouldn't call myself a designer. Tools like Canva and MidJourney became game-changers.

- *Example in Action*: For my AI productivity course, I needed a professional yet approachable presentation design. Canva's templates and AI suggestions helped me create a polished deck that not only looked great but also enhanced my delivery. Attendees later mentioned how much they appreciated the clarity and visuals of the presentation.

Step 3: Automating Repetitive Tasks Workflow management was my next hurdle. With a growing business, repetitive tasks like file organization, email follow-ups, and team updates were eating into my day. That's when I discovered the magic of automation.

- *Example in Action*: Using Zapier, I automated a process where every email attachment was saved to a specific Google Drive folder and shared with my team on Slack. This simple workflow saved hours each week, giving me back precious time to focus on strategy.

Step 4: Scaling Social Media Efforts Social media is a vital part of growing any brand, but managing multiple platforms felt overwhelming. Buffer became my go-to tool for scheduling and analyzing posts, while ChatGPT helped generate fresh content ideas.

- *Example in Action*: I ran an experiment to see which platform drove the most engagement for my course. Using Buffer's analytics and ChatGPT-generated captions tailored to each platform, I optimized my posting schedule. The result? A 35% increase in engagement within the first month.

The Results Within six months, my productivity doubled, and so did my income. The time I saved allowed me to focus on high-impact activities like course development and client consultations. More importantly, the confidence I gained from mastering these tools spilled over into other areas of my business, empowering me to take on challenges I might have avoided before.

Lessons Learned

1. **Start Small**: By focusing on one or two areas at a time, I avoided feeling overwhelmed and saw quick wins that motivated me to continue.

2. **Experiment Boldly**: Not every tool worked for my needs, but testing different approaches helped me discover what clicked.

3. **Integrate Smartly**: The real magic happened when I started combining tools,

like using Canva for visuals that I then shared via Buffer.

Today, I see AI not just as a collection of tools but as a true partner in my business. It's transformed how I work, and I'm excited to help others unlock the same potential.

Actionable Steps to Build Your Toolkit

1. **Start Small**: Choose one tool to solve your biggest problem. Test it for 30 days and evaluate the results.
2. **Learn and Experiment**: Many AI tools offer tutorials or free trials—use them to explore the tool's potential.
3. **Integrate and Scale**: Once you're comfortable, start combining tools (e.g., use Canva for visuals and Buffer for social media).

Conclusion: Your Toolkit is Your Superpower

AI tools aren't just for big companies or tech experts—they're for anyone who wants to work smarter, not harder. By building your AI toolkit, you're equipping yourself to achieve more in less time, freeing you to focus on what truly matters: growing your brand, building relationships, and creating wealth.

In the next chapter, we'll look ahead to the future of AI and explore how you can stay ahead of the curve in this rapidly evolving landscape.

Chapter 12: The Future of AI—Staying Ahead of the Curve

Why the Future is Now

AI is no longer a futuristic concept—it's a present-day revolution reshaping industries, redefining creativity, and reimagining how we live and work. Imagine a world where AI doesn't just assist but collaborates with us in ways we never thought possible. One groundbreaking example is the use of AI in the healthcare industry and with personalized treatment plans. AI-driven healthcare solutions are transforming patient care by analyzing genetic data, medical history, and lifestyle factors to recommend customized treatments. Instead of a one-size-fits-all approach, AI enables doctors to predict which therapies will be most effective for individual patients, improving outcomes and reducing side effects. This shift towards precision medicine is not only enhancing patient care but also accelerating drug discovery, minimizing trial-and-error treatments, and making healthcare more proactive than reactive.

Now, think about your work or business. Where could AI take you over the next decade? Could it help you discover new markets, automate time-consuming tasks, or spark creativity you didn't even know you had? The possibilities are endless—and they're unfolding faster than ever.

As you dive into this chapter, let's embrace a mindset of curiosity and imagination. The future isn't just something to anticipate; it's something you're building today. What role will you play in this rapidly evolving AI landscape? And more importantly, how can you leverage this moment to not just stay ahead but define the curve?

This chapter will guide you through emerging trends, actionable strategies, and ethical considerations to ensure you're equipped for the future of AI. Let's explore the transformative potential of what's next—and how it can amplify your work, your business, and your impact.

The Evolution of AI: What's on the Horizon

The AI tools we've discussed in this book are just the beginning. As technology advances, new opportunities—and challenges—will emerge.

None of us know fully what the future holds, but based on patterns and current advancements, we can glean insights and identify trends that are shaping industries, societies, and individual lives. AI is not just evolving—it's accelerating, bringing innovations that were once the stuff of science fiction into everyday reality. By understanding these trends, you can position yourself to ride the waves of transformation rather than be swept away by them.

Take a moment to imagine: What could your industry or business look like in 10 years if AI continues its rapid evolution? Think of how automated diagnostics in healthcare, immersive learning experiences in education, or hyper-personalized customer interactions might redefine your work. These aren't distant possibilities; they're happening now in experimental forms and scaling fast.

The Evolution of AI: What's on the Horizon (Expanded and Refined)

None of us fully know what the future holds, but based on patterns and current advancements, we can glean insights and identify trends shaping industries, societies, and individual lives. AI is not just evolving—it's accelerating, bringing innovations that were once the stuff of science fiction into everyday reality. By understanding these trends, you can position yourself to ride the waves of transformation rather than be swept away by them.

Imagine how industries could transform in just a few short years. Think of hospitals using AI to predict patient outcomes, online stores offering personalized shopping in real-time, or immersive virtual learning environments. These aren't distant fantasies—they're already happening in experimental forms and scaling fast. Let's explore these transformative trends and see how they'll shape the AI-powered future:

---

1. Hyper-Personalization in Every Industry

AI's ability to tailor products, services, and experiences to individual preferences is expanding rapidly beyond marketing.

- **Example in Action**: A local coffee shop owner leverages AI to customize loyalty offers in real-time, based on a customer's order history and time of day. Customers receive a personalized message like, "Your favorite caramel latte is half-price today!"—boosting foot traffic and sales.
- **Emerging Applications**: Hyper-personalization is already transforming industries like healthcare (personalized treatment plans), education (adaptive learning platforms), and retail (curated shopping experiences).
- **How This Helps Society**: Personalized healthcare saves lives by delivering better

treatments. In education, students thrive when lessons are tailored to their pace and interests.

- **What This Means for You**: Businesses embracing hyper-personalization deepen customer loyalty and drive higher engagement, turning AI into a competitive edge.

---

2. Augmented Reality (AR) and AI Integration

AI-powered augmented reality combines real-world experiences with digital enhancements to reshape industries.

- **Example in Action**: Imagine shopping for furniture online. With AR apps like IKEA Place, users can "place" a sofa in their living room to see how it fits. AI further enhances this by analyzing room dimensions and lighting to make smarter suggestions.
- **Emerging Applications**: AR with AI is being used in interactive training for healthcare (surgical simulations) and manufacturing (assembly line instruction).
- **How This Helps Society**: AR with AI improves safety and accessibility in training

environments, allowing hands-on experience without risks.

- **What This Means for You**: Integrating AR and AI can revolutionize customer experiences, training programs, and even education.

---

3. Autonomous Agents: The Next Frontier

Autonomous agents are AI systems designed to act independently on behalf of users, handling complex tasks without constant supervision.

- **Example in Action**: Meet Alex, a busy entrepreneur who uses AI-powered virtual assistants to handle scheduling, email replies, and even managing parts of their e-commerce store. The agent automatically replenishes inventory, runs A/B ad tests, and provides performance insights—all without Alex lifting a finger.
- **Emerging Applications**: Autonomous agents are being developed in customer service (handling ticketing systems), logistics (supply chain optimization), and productivity tools (calendar management).

- **How This Helps Society**: These agents improve efficiency, reduce human error, and free up time for meaningful work.
- **What This Means for You**: Autonomous agents allow businesses to scale operations while focusing on strategic decision-making.

---

4. Ethical AI and Transparency

As AI grows more powerful, the need for responsible and ethical use becomes increasingly important.

- **Example in Action**: A food delivery platform faced backlash for biased delivery charges in underserved areas. By auditing its algorithms for fairness and publishing the results transparently, the company restored trust and attracted new customers.
- **Emerging Applications**: Ethical AI is being used in recruitment to reduce hiring bias, in finance to ensure fair lending practices, and in public safety for unbiased surveillance.
- **How This Helps Society**: Transparent AI reduces discrimination and ensures fair opportunities across various sectors.

- **What This Means for You**: Emphasizing transparency, fairness, and ethical practices can differentiate your brand in an increasingly AI-driven world.

---

5. Neuro-Symbolic AI: Bridging Logic and Learning

The next wave of AI combines the strengths of symbolic reasoning with deep learning to create smarter, more adaptable systems.

- **Example in Action**: Imagine an AI medical assistant diagnosing a rare disease by combining data-driven symptom analysis with reasoning based on medical literature. The combination of "data" and "logic" enables it to provide both speed and accuracy.
- **Emerging Applications**: Fraud detection in finance, legal case preparation, and enhanced problem-solving in research fields.
- **How This Helps Society**: Neuro-symbolic AI improves safety, accuracy, and efficiency in life-critical fields like healthcare and law.
- **What This Means for You**: Adopting neuro-symbolic AI can lead to breakthroughs

in areas requiring both logical reasoning and vast data interpretation.

6. AI in Healthcare: From Diagnosis to Prevention

AI is revolutionizing healthcare by analyzing complex datasets and predicting outcomes with unmatched precision.

- **Example in Action**: An AI tool analyzes regional health data and flags early signs of an infectious disease outbreak, enabling targeted preventive measures. Meanwhile, hospitals use AI to streamline patient diagnoses by identifying patterns in symptoms.
- **Emerging Applications**: Personalized treatment plans, accelerated drug discovery, and AI-assisted robotic surgeries.
- **How This Helps Society**: AI in healthcare saves lives, reduces costs, and ensures timely interventions in critical situations.
- **What This Means for You**: Entrepreneurs and professionals can harness AI to create healthcare solutions that improve accessibility, affordability, and quality.

---

7. AI-Generated Media: The Content Revolution

AI is transforming how media is created, from art and music to entire video productions.

- **Example in Action**: A marketing agency uses AI to generate engaging visuals for a last-minute campaign. Tools like DALL-E produce high-quality, unique graphics in seconds, while AIVA composes an original soundtrack to tie everything together.
- **Emerging Applications**: Interactive content, personalized advertisements, and AI-generated storytelling are reshaping entertainment and branding.
- **How This Helps Society**: Democratizing content creation empowers small creators to compete with large enterprises, fostering creativity and innovation.
- **What This Means for You**: Staying updated on AI-generated media tools ensures your content remains innovative and competitive in an increasingly saturated market.

Closing Thoughts on Trends

The future of AI is both exciting and uncertain, but one thing is clear: its transformative potential is only beginning to unfold. By staying informed and agile, you can not only adapt to these changes but also harness them to achieve greater creativity, productivity, and impact.

Preparing for the Future: Actionable Steps

To thrive in the future of AI, you need more than just the right tools—you need a mindset of adaptability, curiosity, and innovation. Here's how you can position yourself for success in an AI-driven world:

---

1. Stay Curious and Keep Learning

AI is evolving rapidly, and staying informed is essential to maintaining a competitive edge.

- **Action Step**: Dedicate 30 minutes each week to learning about new AI tools, trends, or breakthroughs. Follow reputable research groups, publications, and industry sources, and observe how patterns are shifting over time.

- **Advanced Tip**: Attend industry conferences or online webinars where you can interact with professionals already using AI to innovate in their fields.
- **Example in Action**: A content creator sets aside time weekly to explore emerging AI platforms, discovering a new tool that automates video editing and saves them hours per project.

---

2. Experiment and Innovate

Innovation often comes from a willingness to step outside your comfort zone and explore uncharted territory.

- **Action Step**: Allocate a small budget or set aside time to test at least one new AI tool or feature each month. Start with tasks where you experience bottlenecks, such as scheduling, marketing, or analytics.
- **Advanced Tip**: Run small-scale experiments within your team or business, and measure the impact of AI tools on efficiency, creativity, or revenue. Use the results to decide which tools to adopt at scale.

- **Example in Action**: A small business owner tests an AI-driven chatbot on their website for one month, discovering it reduces customer inquiry response time by 40%.

---

3. Focus on Adaptability

The ability to pivot and adapt to change will be your greatest asset in a rapidly shifting technological landscape.

- **Action Step**: Create a quarterly review system to assess your current workflows, tools, and strategies. Identify outdated processes that could benefit from automation or enhancement with AI.
- **Advanced Tip**: Cultivate a team culture of adaptability by encouraging employees or collaborators to suggest AI tools or methods that could improve their productivity.
- **Example in Action**: A marketing agency reviews its processes and switches to an AI-powered social media scheduler, freeing up team members to focus on strategy rather than repetitive posting tasks.

---

4. Collaborate with AI Communities

The best ideas often come from collective intelligence, and AI communities can be a goldmine of inspiration and resources.

- **Action Step**: Join online forums like Reddit's *r/MachineLearning*, LinkedIn groups focused on AI, or local meetups where professionals share their experiences and insights.
- **Advanced Tip**: Actively participate by sharing your own use cases or challenges, which can spark valuable discussions and lead to solutions you hadn't considered.
- **Example in Action**: A freelancer joins an AI community and learns about a tool that automates client onboarding, significantly improving their workflow.

---

5. Prioritize Ethical AI Practices

As you integrate AI into your work, ensure you're doing so responsibly and transparently.

- **Action Step**: Regularly audit your use of AI tools to ensure alignment with ethical standards, including data privacy, fairness, and accountability.

- **Advanced Tip**: Develop a public-facing statement about your AI practices to build trust with clients and customers. For example, explain how AI enhances your processes without compromising quality or human oversight.
- **Example in Action**: A nonprofit organization incorporates an ethical AI pledge into their website, boosting donor trust and engagement.

---

6. Build a Long-Term AI Strategy

AI is not just a trend; it's a long-term transformation. Planning for the future ensures you're always ahead of the curve.

- **Action Step**: Develop a roadmap for incorporating AI into your business over the next 1–3 years. Focus on high-impact areas like customer service, content creation, or analytics.
- **Advanced Tip**: Regularly revisit and update your roadmap to account for emerging tools, shifting industry trends, or new opportunities.

- **Example in Action**: A SaaS company creates a 3-year AI adoption plan, identifying milestones for integrating AI into their customer support and product development processes.

Final Thoughts on These Actionable Steps

These steps aren't just about keeping up—they're about getting ahead. By cultivating curiosity, embracing experimentation, and planning strategically, you'll not only adapt to AI's advancements but thrive in this transformative era. The future belongs to those willing to take action today.

Ethical AI: Your Responsibility as a Creator

As AI continues to transform industries and reshape how we work, the responsibility to use it ethically grows. It's no longer enough to focus on what AI can do—we must also consider what it should do. Ethical AI isn't just a nice-to-have; it's a necessity for building trust, fostering integrity, and ensuring fairness in a rapidly evolving technological landscape.

The Stakes of Ethical AI

The rise of AI brings unparalleled opportunities but also raises complex ethical questions. Issues such as bias in algorithms, misuse of AI-generated content, and violations of data privacy can erode trust and lead to unintended consequences.

Story in Action: Imagine a recruitment firm using an AI-powered hiring platform. The algorithm inadvertently favors candidates from certain schools, replicating biases present in its training data. While the tool improves efficiency, its lack of fairness damages the company's reputation and alienates talented candidates.

The ethical use of AI isn't just about avoiding harm, it's about actively creating systems that promote fairness, integrity, objectivity, transparency, and accountability.

Three Pillars of Ethical AI

1. **Fairness:** Avoid bias and promote honest, accurate, and impartial responses, ensuring AI systems deliver unbiased and reliable information.
    - **Example**: A Chat Model or other LLM offers unsolicited commentary on a topic, promoting its own ideological agenda.
    - **Action Step**: AI models should be unbiased in their responses and answers. They should be data-driven responses without embedding ideological agendas or personal preferences. Promoting objectivity, trust, goodwill, and equality.
2. **Accountability** Those developing, programming, training, and encoding AI models should adhere to ethical standards and best practices, actively addressing concerns when they arise. This includes publicly acknowledging and taking responsibility for errors caused by their AI system, as well as implementing measures to resolve issues and prevent future occurrences.

- **Example**: A social media platform uses AI to review and approve advertisements. The algorithm mistakenly rejects ads from small businesses selling perfectly legitimate products, such as handmade crafts or cultural clothing, labeling them as "violating community standards."
- **Action Step**: Publicly recognizing that the AI's moderation unfairly impacted small businesses and apologizing for the inconvenience. Then as stated before, providing transparency and offering solutions, and then using that information to improve systems goes a long way to building trust.

3. **Privacy and Security:** Respecting user data is non-negotiable. AI systems often require significant data inputs, but it's your responsibility to handle this data ethically and securely.
   - **Example**: A small business adopts an AI email marketing platform that anonymizes recipient data while still providing actionable insights.

- **Action Step**: Use AI tools that prioritize data encryption and anonymization. Avoid collecting unnecessary personal information.

Practical Steps for Ethical AI Implementation

1. **Audit Your AI Tools:** Regularly review how your AI tools process data, make decisions, and generate outputs. This helps identify and address potential ethical pitfalls.
   - **Advanced Tip**: Partner with third-party auditors or ethical AI consultants for unbiased assessments of your tools.
2. **Educate Your Team:** Ethical AI is a team effort. Ensure that everyone involved in using AI understands the importance of responsible practices.
   - **Action Step**: Host workshops or provide training on ethical AI practices for your team or collaborators.
3. **Engage Your Audience:** Building trust means involving your audience in the

conversation. Solicit feedback on how your AI practices align with their values.

- **Example**: A nonprofit surveys its donors about how AI should be used to enhance transparency and efficiency in its campaigns.

Case Study: Ethical AI in Action

A retail company faced backlash after its AI-powered recommendation engine disproportionately promoted male-oriented products to all users, regardless of their preferences. Recognizing the issue, the company conducted a thorough audit and retrained its AI using diverse and balanced datasets. It also created a transparent report explaining the changes and invited customers to participate in shaping future improvements. The result? Restored trust and increased customer engagement.

Why Ethical AI Matters to You

Ethical AI isn't just about avoiding controversy—it's a strategic advantage. Businesses and creators that prioritize ethics build stronger relationships, stand out in competitive markets, and contribute to a more equitable future.

Looking Forward: The Role of Ethics in AI Innovation

As AI continues to evolve, the importance of ethics will only grow. By committing to accountability, transparency, integrity, fairness, and privacy, you can lead by example, setting a standard for others to follow. Ethical AI isn't a limitation; it's an opportunity to create technology that truly serves humanity.

The Human Element: Why You Still Matter

Despite its transformative power, AI will never replace human creativity, empathy, or vision. Your role as a creator, entrepreneur, or business owner is to guide the technology, ensuring it amplifies your unique strengths rather than diminishing them.

When I first started using AI, I feared it might make my skills redundant. But over time, I realized that AI isn't a replacement—it's a partner. It streamlines my workflow, inspires new ideas, and frees me to focus on what I do best: connecting with people and sharing my vision. AI is powerful, but the human element remains irreplaceable.

Looking Ahead: The Next Steps for You

The future of AI is exciting, but the real question is: how will you leverage it? Here's your roadmap for staying ahead:

1. **Commit to Lifelong Learning**: AI is a journey, not a destination. Stay curious and keep exploring.
2. **Embrace Change**: Be open to new tools, strategies, and opportunities as they arise.
3. **Take Action Today**: Whether it's trying a new tool or rethinking your approach to branding, the best way to prepare for the future is to start now.

The Future of AI

AI is transforming the world at a pace we've never seen before, offering endless opportunities to innovate, grow, and make a lasting impact. But the true power of AI doesn't come from the tools themselves—it comes from how you choose to use them. With the insights, strategies, and tools shared in this book, you're now equipped to lead, create, and thrive in this era of unprecedented technological advancement.

Take a moment to reflect on the journey you've taken through these chapters. You've learned how to overcome common myths, navigate biases, and embrace AI as a partner in your entrepreneurial and creative pursuits. You've explored a rich toolkit of technologies that can save time, amplify your efforts, and open doors to new possibilities. Most importantly, you've gained the mindset needed to adapt, experiment, and grow in a world that rewards innovation.

But knowledge is only the first step. The real transformation happens when you take action. Start small—experiment with a single tool or apply one strategy to improve your workflow. Build momentum by integrating AI into your daily routines. Celebrate the wins, learn from the challenges, and always remain curious about what's next.

The future isn't just about staying ahead of the curve; it's about shaping the curve. Whether you're a solopreneur, a creative professional, or a leader of a growing business, the potential of AI is yours to harness. Imagine what's possible when you combine human ingenuity with the power of AI—how your ideas can grow, your influence can expand, and your impact can resonate far beyond what you once thought possible.

As you close this book, remember: this is just the beginning. The tools and insights you now hold are the foundation for a journey of innovation and success. If you're ready to take the next step, consider exploring my online course, where we dive even deeper into actionable strategies and advanced techniques. Or simply start your first AI-driven project today—the future is waiting for you to create it.

So go ahead. Build. Innovate. Thrive. The next chapter of your journey begins now.

Conclusion

Benjamin Franklin, one of the Founding Fathers of the United States, was a visionary whose words continue to inspire generations. Known for his wisdom, ingenuity, and relentless pursuit of progress, Franklin once said, *"An investment in knowledge pays the best interest."* This quote resonates profoundly in our era, where knowledge is not just power but a catalyst for transformation. The tools and strategies you've learned in this book are your investment in knowledge, poised to yield dividends in the form of success, growth, and fulfillment.

In this book, we hope you've seen that we live in one of the greatest times in human history. The opportunity provided by AI and web technologies is unprecedented, enabling you to achieve goals that once seemed out of reach. Whether you're a solopreneur looking to scale, a creative pursuing your passion, or a business owner seeking new ways to grow, the resources at your fingertips are revolutionary. The question is, will you seize the moment?

Before we part ways—and before you close this book—I want to remind you of something crucial: success is not about perfection; it's about progress.

Each step you take toward implementing what you've learned is a step closer to realizing your potential. The journey may seem daunting, but you're not alone. Together, we're navigating this exciting frontier.

The Biggest Misconceptions of Leveraging AI Technology

Misconception 1: AI Does All the Work

Leveraging AI technologies may appear like everything will be done for you. However, the reality is that AI is a tool, not a replacement for your effort. It's here to amplify your capabilities, not eliminate the need for your creativity and decision-making. Think of AI as an assistant, one that thrives when guided by a thoughtful and intentional leader—you.

Misconception 2: The Work is Effortless

People underestimate the amount of work it takes. The allure of automation often creates a misconception that results come effortlessly. The truth? Success requires you to learn the tools, craft strategies, and consistently execute your vision. AI makes the process easier, but the foundation is built on your dedication and perseverance.

Hard-Earned Wisdom

After working with thousands of clients and hundreds of business owners over the past 25 years, I have seen a recurring pattern. Those who succeed don't wait for opportunities—they create them. They use AI not as a crutch, but as a catalyst, blending technology with their unique human touch.

Misconception 3: AI is a Magic Wand

Many people think AI will just do everything for them and open some magical door to their success. Unfortunately, this is a misconception—or fortunately, depending on how you look at it. You want to convey your true self, your authentic business. AI can streamline and optimize, but your creativity and personal touch bring the heart and soul to what you do.

A Proven Process

When people stumble upon my articles or videos on AI and web technology, they often don't realize how much experience and experimentation has shaped my perspective. Over time, I've developed strategies that blend AI with human ingenuity, creating a formula for sustainable success.

A Winning Formula

Through determination, commitment, the right strategy, and perseverance, you can achieve remarkable results. In this book, we've given you the steps to get started. Now it's up to you to take action, adapt to the challenges, and seize the opportunities that await.

In Chapter 3 on Strategy, I gave you part of our AI Web Accelerator Framework, the MOVE FAST framework. It was a play on words, by you making a *fast move,* you can *move fast* to your destination. This high-level jumpstart is part of a larger system designed to help you achieve your goals. From setting up funnels and leveraging AI to outreach and traffic optimization, you now have the tools to grow your brand and income. Remember, AI is here to support you, but your vision and execution make the difference.

By now, you see that this takes a lot of work, but it is still a lot easier—and your load is lighter—by leveraging these tools. With AI and web strategies, you have the power to create impact while freeing up time to focus on what matters most.

Time is of the Essence

We have never seen a time like this in human history, where you can create anything—a video, an image, or an entire strategy—out of thin air, with just the words you type on a keyboard. The barriers to entry are lower than ever, and the possibilities are endless.

It's up to you to leverage these tools and this time for your own benefit. The window of opportunity is wide open, but it won't stay that way forever. The time to act is now.

The Future Awaits

The future is unknown, but one thing is certain: those who embrace change and innovate will thrive. AI and web strategies are the keys to navigating this evolving landscape. Don't wait for the perfect moment; take advantage of this opportunity and see where it can take you and your business.

Keep on Learning and Growing

While this book may be coming to an end, the work of learning and adaptation does not.

AI and modern technology are evolving quickly, and no single person, platform, or method holds all the answers. Continued growth comes from staying engaged with new thinking, following practitioners who are shaping the field, and learning alongside others who understand that adopting intelligent systems is not just a technical step, but an organizational and strategic shift.

Staying True to Your Vision

Always remember why you started. AI can lighten your workload, but it can't replace your vision. You are the captain of your ship, the architect of your success. Keep serving your audience and staying true to your purpose.

Final Words

In this book, you've learned how to harness AI and web strategies to build your income, influence, and impact. Now it's time to put that knowledge into action. The road ahead is yours to define. Take what you've learned, keep experimenting, and let your passion guide you.

The future belongs to those who are willing to embrace it. Go out there, make your mark, and create the success you've always envisioned.

About The Author

STEVE KLEIN is the Founder and CEO of Zareco Inc., an advisory firm focused on enterprise AI strategy and systems thinking. With more than three decades of experience spanning software development, enterprise platforms, and emerging AI technologies, his career reflects the full evolution of the modern digital landscape — from early internet infrastructure through today's large language models.

His work has consistently focused on one core question: how do intelligent systems reshape the way organizations and individuals work, communicate, and make decisions?

AI Tech Secrets is the practical expression of that focus — a straightforward guide for business owners, professionals, and teams looking to work smarter using AI and automation. It cuts through the hype to deliver actionable frameworks and real-world applications that save time, increase output, and build the kind of operational clarity that compounds over time.

Steve brings a systems-oriented approach that emphasizes long-term thinking and practical integration over trend-driven adoption. He lives in the Pacific Northwest with his family, where he continues to work at the intersection of applied AI, systems design, and the future of modern work.

Made in the USA
Monee, IL
04 November 2026

67385837R00138